1

OFFSIDE

- A Memoir -

Challenges Faced by Women in Hockey

Rhonda Leeman Taylor

And Denbeigh Whitmarsh

Written by Rhonda Leeman Taylor
and Denbeigh Whitmarsh.

Cover and interior artwork designed by and property of Marlon Lahens.

Copyright © Rhonda Taylor 2019.

ISBN: 978-1-9992323-1-3 (Paperback)
ISBN: 978-1-9992323-0-6 (E-Book)

For every book purchased, a portion of the proceeds will be donated to the Grindstone Award Foundation *to support young girls in hockey.*

About Grindstone Award:

The Grindstone Award Foundation is a registered Canadian charity that provides opportunities to young female hockey players who have a desire to play, but are unable to due to financial reasons. Our vision is to lead and inspire the movement to grow female hockey across the nation.

"Rhonda Leeman Taylor's "OFFSIDE" story offers honest and needed perspectives from a pivotal time in the development of women's hockey. While it may be difficult for today's young players to truly grasp the challenges faced by Rhonda (and countless other pioneers of the women's game), it is important to share these solemn accounts and celebratory victories in order to really appreciate the progress that has been realized and the efforts that are still needed for all players to enjoy equitable opportunities and lifelong enjoyment of the great game of hockey. Thank you Rhonda for sharing your memoir and for skillfully stickhandling your way through so many hurdles!"

Dr. Denyse Lafrance Horning
Women's Hockey Researcher
Nipissing University

"Thank you, Rhonda for your courage, determination and continued perseverance to make women's ice hockey a level playing field. The trials and tribulations that you have endured throughout your career are full of resiliency. Your passion for the success of our beloved, thriving game is encouraging to the future generations yet to come. You are an empowering role model for us all. Thank you!

May the torch burn brighter than ever as we continue to shine light on and overcome inequalities!"

Pro Coach Tatjana "Tiki" Tikhonov
Granddaughter of Viktor Tikhonov
Owner of Tikhonov Training Camp

"In OFFSIDE, *Rhonda Leeman-Taylor draws upon her personal experiences to tell the story of systemic change in female hockey during the past five decades. We come to see how the resiliency of early advocates laid the foundation for the women's hockey model we have today. The growth of the game has not been easy – involving ongoing tension between the strong sense of community among the women and girls who play and entrenched male-dominated governance and competitive structures. Through Rhonda's account we learn how to face adversity and build a game you love. Let's now move the puck up the ice!"*

Dr. Julie Stevens
Hockey Player, Coach, Advocate, Organizer,
And Scholar at Brock University

"Rhonda is an inspiration in her achievements in all things; and we love how her passion and dedication to making a difference to women's sports visibility is also evident in all that she commits to. She is legendary with what she can achieve, and her work in this field was so far ahead of its time that we are only just getting to see other sporting codes and countries following her challenge. We are proud to have her on the team, now making a difference to inclusive career experiences!"

Anne Fulton
Founder, Fuel50 CareerPathing

Being picked by the Edmonton Chimos to play in the first Shopper's Drug Mart National Championships in 1982 was an honour in itself. To find out that there was a National Championship tournament being held in Brantford, Ontario brought a level of excitement for my love of the game that I could not have imagined. Not only was this the first Nationals but it was being held in the hometown of my hockey hero, Wayne Gretzky.

A year earlier I was fortunate enough to play in the Brampton Four Rinks tournament representing my hometown of Wainwright, Alberta, in the "B" division. At one point I had the opportunity to watch some of the women on the "A" side. At that moment I set a goal for myself that one day I would play at the highest level possible. Being a part of the first Nationals was it!

The tournament was very well organized to a degree that a budding hockey player was completely privileged to be a part of. Knowing that a big corporation such as Shopper's Drug Mart was the main sponsor felt like we had finally made it as hockey athletes; we were finally being recognized for our sport. Compound that with my opportunity to score the first goal of this championship. A trophy consisting of the puck was sent off to the Hockey Hall of Fame.

Fast forward 22 years later and I was selected on Team Canada to participate in the 1994 World Championships in Lake Placid, New York where we returned home with the gold medal. The Women's National Championships set the tone and the scene for more hockey to come. Canada was introduced to the first big wave of elite hockey players who would go on to grow the game to where it is at today.

Jane Lagacé
Former Member of Team Canada
(Women's Hockey)

Table of Contents

To the volunteers and players the world has never known.

In The Beginning

I was about six. I saw my brother Glenn building a fort across the schoolyard. I didn't think twice but went over to the boys' side of the playground to join in his fun. Mind you, it wasn't much fun afterwards when I received the leather strap across my palms in front of my classmates for having been a girl

playing a boys' game,
on the boys' turf.

***

In my youth, I delivered my brothers' newspaper routes for them when they had hockey or football practice. Eventually, I ended up delivering the paper full-time in their place. After a few years, my mother decided to have the contract transferred to my name. But the paper director found out that a girl had been doing a boy's job.

He told us girls were not welcome in the position because the papers were too heavy for us to carry.

***

Children are supposed to trust their elders. But when a guidance counsellor suggested that I join the Armed Forces to "learn to conform," to get the discipline I needed to "fit in," that is, to fit into the model of the perfect female that society expected me to become,

I left his office. In anger.

Preface

Women have never had it easy in the sports world. We've been deprived of financial equality, peppered with insults, even legally mandated out of teams – all on the basis of a single X chromosome. Our so-called "limitations" have been keeping us out of professional sports leagues, out of equal playing opportunities, out of equal salaries and media coverage, and the list goes on.

As a young girl in Canada in the 1960s, I witnessed blatant discrimination. As an older woman in the 21st century, the discrimination is less visible but still highly effective. I'd hoped that by this point in my life women would have achieved equal status with men. I still have hope that we will do so within my lifetime.

I started playing hockey in 1969 when I was in grade 10. Back then, there were very few girls who played the game, but those of us who did play did so out of pure love for the sport. One can only imagine the passion required to hurdle the social barriers restricting our access to what was then seen as a "man's game," and then to hold our positions while fighting through a barrage of insults and ignorance.

Hockey was, and still is, one of the most important parts of my life. Over the years, I've been a player, a referee, a coach, a coach's coach, an administrator, and always a fan. Hockey is how I made many of my closest friends, how I connected on a deeper level with family members, and how I met my husband of 36 years.

I truly love hockey. Hockey, however, has not always loved me.

In 2004, I suffered a life-altering spinal injury while playing in a pickup women's league. I was forced to sue Hockey Canada for the money I needed for treatment, and to replace a significant amount of lost income as chronic pain reduced my ability to focus long enough to hold down a job. My husband and I had to downsize our house to a wheelchair-accessible bungalow in case my spinal condition worsens with age. And yet, this isn't the most difficult blow that hockey dealt me.

My prime years of involvement as an administrator began in the late 1970s, when I was hired by Hockey Ontario to develop a league for women in the province, becoming their first ever paid female employee. In 1982, I was chair of the first official National Women's Hockey Championship in Canada, an event that would pave the way for women to reach the international stage in the early 1990s.

After the Nationals, I was elected as the first chair of the Female Council, an organization that is still the governing body for women's hockey in Canada today. Thanks to this, I became the first woman to sit on Hockey Canada's Board of Directors, obtained voting rights, and successfully fought to remove body checking from the women's game.

But I would not stay in these important positions for long. My career in hockey administration was cut short due to adversity from a few members of the organizational team. To me, the inability to further assist in the promotion of the women's game was a bigger hit than the one that caused my spinal injury.

I hope that by writing this memoir I can still contribute to the advancement of women's equality in sport despite my current distance from the hockey governing body. I believe that this book will help bring to light some of the more intimate details of the discrimination and other difficulties faced by women like myself on both the administrative and player sides of the sporting world. I hope that it will incite both the women *and* the men of the future to take up the torch in the battle against gender inequality.

I'm not telling my story because it is unique; I'm telling it because I know there are thousands of other women out there who have faced and overcome challenges similar to my own. I do not aim to speak *for* these women, but rather, *beside* them.

Let us stand in solidarity and remember our past as we prepare to face a new era of adversity, and of progress.

A Short History of Women's Hockey in Canada

"And there is fear…
They told us that if the women won,
the boys would be psychologically scarred for life." [1]

For most of the 19th and 20th centuries, too many Western chauvinists viewed female athletes as "controversial" or "wrong," and upheld numerous misconceptions about women in sport. These include the notion that women "belong in the home," that sports may damage their "delicate bodies," or even that hockey will remove their *"polish,"* making them *"leather-limbed and inclined to flat chests,"* as suggested by journalist Andy Lytle in 1913.[2]

Women in hockey have been facing this kind of backlash since the birth of the game in the late 1800s. Yet despite this

---

[1] Rhonie Horne, quoted in Scanlon, Kevin. "Sibling Rivalry Can Inspire Girls on Ice," *The Toronto Star* [Toronto], 20 Dec. 1981.
[2] Comment made by Andy Lytle, journalist for the *Vancouver Sun,* 1913; quoted in McFarlane, Brian. *Proud Past, Bright Future: One Hundred Years of Canadian Women's Hockey.* Toronto, Stoddart, 1994, p. 49.

Victorian prejudice, hockey gained substantially in popularity among women in North America during the 20th century.

The earliest records of women in hockey date back to the 1880s. Photographs from that time show both men and women playing the game at skating parties hosted by Lord and Lady Stanley at Rideau Hall, with the women playing in full skirts![3] The first documented organized women's game occurred in 1889 between the Government house team (featuring Lord Stanley's daughter Isobel), and the Rideau Ladies, just 14 years after the first documented men's game in 1875.[4]

These women hockey players were among thousands to join teams over the next few decades, alongside an increasing number of females who rebelled against patriarchal values and entered a variety of sports which had been previously reserved for men.[5] In the case of the freshly-invented sport of ice hockey, the women's game expanded nearly simultaneously to that of the men.[6]

In other words, women playing hockey is nothing new.

The turn of the century would see the creation of women's varsity hockey teams in universities such as McGill, Laval, Queen's, and the University of Toronto, all part of LOHA (the Ladies' Ontario Hockey Association).[7] These teams were good enough (and

[3] McFarlane, *Proud Past, Bright Future*, p. 4.
[4] McFarlane, *Proud Past, Bright Future*, p. 7; Vigneault, Michel. *La Naissance d'un sport organisé au Canada: le hockey à Montréal, 1875-1917*. Thesis, Université Laval, Quebec, July 2001, p. 84.
[5] Hall, Ann. *The Girl and the Game*, University of Toronto Press, 2017, p. 27.
[6] Vigneault, *La Naissance d'un sport organisé au Canada*, p. 84.
[7] McFarlane, *Proud Past, Bright Future*, p. 63.

entertaining enough) to warrant charging admission, with the teams making as much as $50 per game.8

Many women also joined leagues outside of universities and often admission charges would be donated to charity.9 Up until the Second World War, Canadian women were able to compete for the Eastern and Western Canada titles (in most years), and the winners would have a shot at "National" glory in the Dominion Championships.10

An article from 1911 in *The Nugget*, from Cobalt, Ontario, reports over 1,000 fans turning out to watch a local women's game.11 Likewise, the infamous Preston Rivulettes (who maintained a win-loss record of 348 wins to only 2 losses, the all-time best ratio in either men's or women's hockey history) reportedly drew over 6,000 fans to one of their matches in Galt, Ontario, in 1935.12

The sport's increase in popularity prior to the war proves that women's hockey was not simply an entertaining novelty item, but that the players had developed a sound and lasting skill that was appreciated by their many spectators. In fact, in the late 1930's, the Preston Rivulettes had even planned a hockey tour through Europe to

8 Manning, Sally. *A Golden Tear: Danièle Sauvageau's Journey to Olympic Gold.* Toronto, CNIB, 2004, p. 14; McFarlane, *Proud Past, Bright Future*, p. 16, 27.
9 McFarlane, *Proud Past, Bright Future*, p. 24.
10 Although it should be noted that these "Dominion" tournaments were neither comprehensive nor reliable, and weren't really representative of the apogee of female skill in the country at the time since many players were restricted from competition by financial and social barriers, as well as by the disparity between the sexes in the distribution of resources and icetime.
11 Quoted in McFarlane, *Proud Past, Bright Future*, p. 41.
12 Etue, Elizabeth, and Megan K. Williams. *On the Edge: Women Making Hockey History.* EPUB ed., Toronto, Second Story Press, 1999, p. 41-43.

showcase their skills overseas and promote global interest in the sport, in an attempt to include women's hockey in the Olympic Games. Unfortunately, this tour was cancelled due to the onset of WWII.13

Yet despite this strong fanbase, it seems that the rebellious women of the early 1900s were not supported by many sections of the population. This view is documented in the numerous conservative opinions in news articles published in the 1910s and 20s (again, the very idea that women need be *"polished"* makes my insides writhe in anger), and even by the name of the first Queen's University team, the *Love-Me-Littles*.14

It appears that this era saw sports rise in popularity among its high-spirited youth despite the wishes of some of their more traditional counterparts. This situation sounded all too familiar to those of us trying to increase the popularity of the sport in the early 1980s.

How is it that a battalion of defiant young women in ankle-length skirts back in the 1880s (or with the slight upgrade to bloomers after 1917), so highly resembled the insurgency of poofy-haired girls begging for icetime almost a century later? How is it that the gender discrimination faced by both these groups so closely matches that

---

13 "History," *Rivulettes Junior Hockey Club,* Cambridge City Archives, http://rivuletteshockey.pointstreaksites.com/view/rivuletteshockey/history. Accessed 1 Sept. 2019; See also Power, Tracey. *Glory.* 26 July 2019, Thousand Islands Playhouse. Theatrical Performance. (A very good rendition of the incredible story of the Preston Rivulettes).
14 McFarlane, *Proud Past, Bright Future*, p. 16.

faced by the girls playing national- and international-level hockey today?

The problem ultimately lies in the culture shift that occurred in Western society following the Second World War. During the 1940s and '50s, women's hockey was largely put on hold in favour of the war effort. Very few women's teams remained operational. This era would also see the NHL suffer the loss of nearly its entire roster, to be replaced by underage boys and military rejects. However, the men's game continued to be aired on radio and covered by the media, apparently to "boost morale" for the fighting population. In contrast, the women's game almost never reached the newspapers or airwaves.[15]

At the end of the war, the NHL came back stronger than ever, and it would even be televised starting in 1952.[16] But the progress made by women's rights activists in the first half of the century was halted, and even reversed, after the men returned from overseas and demanded that women abandon the work world and return to the kitchen. The same was demanded of women who had entered the sports world, and it would take until the 1980s for women's hockey to be considered as "socially acceptable" as it had been in the 1930s.

The fact that the general acceptance of women's hockey could fluctuate so dramatically only proves the extent to which the game's public support is a cultural construct and has absolutely nothing to do with the women's level of skill. It's also interesting that the men's

15 McFarlane, *Proud Past, Bright Future*, p. 107.
16 Etue and Williams, *On the Edge*, p. 41-42.

game should grow in success when it reached the public via radio and television, while the unadvertised women's game would proportionally decrease in popularity.

There is an important story that I'd like to share that epitomizes the general sentiment towards females in hockey in the post-war period. It's the story of Abby Hoffman, a four-time Olympic distance runner who later became the director of Sport Canada.

As a nine-year-old girl in 1956, Abby enrolled herself in a boys' league under the name "Ab Hoffman," as there were no girls' teams near her home. Her superior skill level along with her short-cropped hair allowed her to play nearly an entire season unnoticed.[17] Her ploy was only discovered after she was selected for the league's all-star team and her coach had to double check her birth certificate. [18] She was immediately asked to leave the program despite having been chosen only days before as the team's best player.

A similar case occurred in 1977 when 11-year-old goalie Gail Cummings was kicked off a competitive boys' team in Huntsville, Ontario. Gail's mother Dorothy proceeded to take the issue to the Ontario Human Rights Commission, arguing that it was against the Charter of Rights and Freedoms for Gail to be denied access to a social service purely on the basis of sex.

Initially, the court determined that Dorothy's case was justified and mandated that the Ontario Minor Hockey Association

[17] McFarlane, *Proud Past, Bright Future*, p. 117-118.
[18] The coach allegedly called Abby's mother, claiming that "Ab" had brought in his sister's certificate by accident.

allow Gail to play with her male peers. The OMHA, however, was not happy with this decision and asked their teams to boycott girl players, and even boycott games against teams with girls on their rosters in other provinces and countries.

The OMHA proceeded to call for an appeal and sadly won their case in the Supreme Court of Ontario, revoking Gail's right to play with the boys.[19] Unfortunately, in both Gail and Abby's cases (and as in many more), the question debated by the court was not whether this was a sexist decision, but rather, whether the sport program was considered public or private, which determined if it had to abide by the Canadian Charter of Rights and Freedoms on gender discrimination.[20]

The period in which these two incidents originated is roughly where my story starts. This memoir will cover the years from the late 1960s to the early 1980s, during which time I was first a player, then an administrator and a coach. It was during my childhood in the '60s and '70s that public interest in women's hockey began to slowly resurface, and hundreds of girls like Gail and Abby were forced to sharpen their elbows in order to take part in the sport they loved.

I shared in this challenging collective journey and faced no shortage of insults and obstacles in the process. It's only thanks to the resiliency of the women of the 1960s and '70s that females today can

19 McFarlane, *Proud Past, Bright Future*, p. 114-177.
20 Hall, M. Ann, and Dorothy A. Richardson. *Fair Ball: Towards Sex Equality in Canadian Sport.* Ottawa, Canadian Advisory Council on the Status of Women, 1982, p. 19.

play hockey, be it on the local boys' team or in a competitive girls' league of their own.

Other Fun Facts about the History of Women's Hockey

- The first goalie facemask in hockey was worn by Elizabeth Graham on the Queen's University team in 1927, 32 years before Jacques Plante would stun the hockey world with the "introduction" of the facemask to (men's) hockey in 1959.[21] Rumour has it that Elizabeth had recently had some dental work done and didn't want to risk damaging her pricey new smile.[22]

- Some of the earliest female goalies would sew buckshot into the hems of their full-length skirts, using their weighted dresses to stop low-sliding pucks from entering the net![23]

- In the first decade of the 1900s, many women's teams, such as a team from Trois-Rivières, Québec, would only play in indoor arenas and refused entry to all men for the duration of their icetime out of fear that their skirts would fly up if they fell down.[24]

[21] McFarlane, *Proud Past, Bright Future*, p. 70.
[22] Norris, Mike. "Queen's goalie made history by donning mask." *The Kingston Whig Standard* [Kingston], 19 Feb. 2016, https://www.thewhig.com/2016/02/19/queens-goalie-made-history-by-donning-mask/wcm/9f40a766-8200-3fd4-8faa-fd207c51974d. Accessed 3 Sept. 2019.
[23] McFarlane, *Proud Past, Bright Future*, p. 30.
[24] McFarlane, *Proud Past, Bright Future*, p. 16.

- The invention of the sports bra, the jill strap (female jock strap), and the women's chest protector by Cooper and CCM in the late 1970s gave women better access to the game by protecting against breast and pelvic injuries. There was a common misconception at the time that such injuries would cause cancer for women in the "delicate" areas affected. This misconception was often used as an excuse to keep girls from playing the sport.

Growing Up in Sports in the '60s and '70s

I am the youngest of seven children born to Ed and Ellen Marie Leeman. Our family lived in a small house in Kingston, Ontario, only a few blocks from Victoria Park. My father worked long hours at the local Alcan (aluminum) plant, and my mother juggled raising her five daughters and two sons while working part time as a supply teacher.

Growing up, I was aware that we were a "hockey family," and that my parents were dedicated volunteers. My father was a member of the Catholic school board for nearly 20 years, and my mother seemed to always be baking for a charity or non-profit organization. Both Ed and Ellen Marie also put in countless hours raising funds for my brothers' hockey team, the Kingston Royals, which was part of the Kingston Amateur Hockey Association back then.

My parents would often help host high school dance events to raise travel money for their sons' teams. I can recall one of these events, which turned out to be quite a success since the unknown band they had hired a year in advance was none other than *The Guess*

Who, and the band had grown to be very successful just in time for our (now sold-out) high school dance!

In our younger years, my siblings and I spent most of our summers running around at our cottage on Loughborough Lake, just north of Kingston. In the winters, we spent days on end playing hockey. I suppose I learned to skate and handle the puck from my brothers.

I would often play shinny with my brother Glenn in the hallways of the Memorial Arena in Kingston while my brother Ed was at practice. There was one hallway in that building where you could always find a pile of broken hockey sticks, which worked great for a scrimmage with a rolled-up paper ball or an old puck. I remember Don Cherry telling me a few years ago that he would always remember the snotty-nosed Leeman kids playing in the hallways of that arena during the years he coached.

My brother Ed was a talented hockey player, and my father was ever so proud of his son. Ed was the leading goal scorer in his league, and many believed he could have been drafted to the NHL if he had been interested in playing professionally. Two of his peers – Dennis Kearns and Syl Apps – went on to become successful NHL players and Hall of Famers, although in their youth, Ed was incontestably the best of the three.

In terms of outdoor hockey, we alternated between shinny on the backyard rink of our neighbours (the Pushcars) and playing on the local outdoor rink in Victoria Park. When we played on the Pushcars' ice, I remember we would usually go outside around 9 or 10 in the morning. We wouldn't take our skates off when we came in for lunch. Instead, Mum would lay sheets of cardboard across the linoleum floor so we could come inside with our blades on, eat our soup and sandwich, and then head right back out again to play until dark. I think this is where I learned to be a good skater, which became one of my strengths during my later years as a player. It didn't take long to learn that if you couldn't skate well, you had to be goalie, and if you were goalie, you would freeze to death on that outdoor rink!

When we played at Victoria Park, when I was really little, my mother didn't trust me to walk to the park and change into my skates by myself. Luckily, our road was part of the bus route, and since the city didn't put salt on the roads in those days, the buses would have usually worn down the snow into glare ice that you could glide along right to the rink! If not, I'd have to walk in my skates along the neighbours' front lawns a block and a half to the rink, and then crawl across the pavement patches on my hands and knees to avoid dulling my blades!

Once at the rink, I admit that I was often insecure about my hockey skills, and I didn't feel like I fit in well with the general community. In Victoria Park, I would only play hockey with the boys if the rink was sparsely populated that day. If there were too many people, I would ditch the stick and opt for a recreational skate around the ice with the rest of the girls.

Sometimes I would tuck my hair up under my toque to avoid being recognized as female, as my bulky coat and mitts hid the rest of my features well. This disguise allowed me to be picked far higher in

31

the draft, as the captains, usually young men from Queen's, couldn't identify my gender. Naturally, I wanted to be chosen sooner and I wasn't opposed to sacrificing my image to make that happen. After I had been selected, I would drop my hair out from under my toque and play with it flowing in the wind for the rest of the game, damn proud to be a girl who knew how to play hockey.

Back in those times, it was so important to act "lady-like," although I never really understood why. We were a very Catholic family and I was taught by nuns in the separate school system. I don't believe I was ever well-liked by any of the sisters, probably because I had a hard time following a lot of their rules.

I recall one day, when I was about six years old, I saw my brother Glenn building a fort on the other side of the schoolyard. I didn't think twice but went right on over to the boys' side of the playground to join in his fun. Mind you, it wasn't much fun afterwards when I received the leather strap across my palms for having played with the boys. As a young girl, I had trouble wrapping my mind around why I could play with my brothers at home but not at school. That a girl *must* remain prim and proper and miss out on forts and other "boys' activities" is a concept I still have a hard time comprehending today.

Growing up as a "tomboy," I absolutely worshipped my two older brothers Ed and Glenn. Age-wise, they were the closest to me of all my siblings and I wanted to do everything they did. I wanted to play their games, which looked so much more fun than playing house and Barbies. I never wanted to wear my shirt at the cottage because they didn't have to wear their shirts. I even used to deliver my brother's paper route for them when they had hockey or football practice, and I eventually ended up delivering it for them full time for a few years, until my mother decided to have the contract transferred into my name.

At this point, the paper director found out that a girl had been doing the boys' job and wouldn't let me keep the position any longer because apparently it would be "too heavy" for a girl to carry the 112 papers around our neighbourhood. Little did he know that not even my older brothers had wanted to carry that weight, and that we all simply pulled it on a wagon behind us!

At 15, I obtained my gun licence just to follow my father and brothers out into the woods on their frequent hunting trips. Later, I would also organize a target shooting club for women. We practiced our skills twice a week in the basement of our school, which had doubled as a cadet training facility following the war. I even went so far as teaching myself to pee through a toilet paper roll when I was about five or six, just so I could urinate standing up like my brothers!

I think a lot of these desires arose from the attention I saw my parents give to my male siblings. In our house, in terms of sports, all efforts were put towards the boys. They received the new equipment, the fundraising help, the drives to games and practices, and most importantly, the praise. My parents dragged me along to all of their sons' hockey games, and even though I thoroughly enjoyed watching my brothers, I couldn't help but be envious of the fantastic opportunity they had been given. I saw the attention they were getting and the fun they were having, and I wanted in.

It was during one of these games that I saw the Queen's University women's team glide off the rink. I was about 12 years old, and it was the first time I'd ever seen women's hockey played in an organized league. I knew in a second that I wanted to be on a team like that.

I'd played women's basketball and a few other organized sports up until that point, and I figured I was a good skater and could handle the puck well, thanks to playing with my brothers. I decided I'd try and find a women's team to play on. I determined in that moment that I needed to go to university – not to get a degree, but to play girls' hockey!

At that point in my life, no one in my family had yet attended a university full time, so I knew my chances of playing on the Queen's team would be pretty slim. But thankfully, I didn't have to wait until my post-secondary education to play on a women's team. In 1969, my second year of high school, I read an advertisement in the *Kingston Whig Standard* about a group of women who were looking for players to form their own community team, and I knew I had found my calling.

In the beginning, my parents were skeptical about my decision to play hockey in a women's league, believing it was no more than a passing whim. But that was of little importance to me because this was something that *I* wanted to do for myself, whether they chose to support me or not. So a few days later, I took the bus alone to go and try my hand at playing for the Red Barons.

I was 15, wildly excited, and equally unprepared. I had never played an official game of hockey before, only shinny with my brothers. I didn't even have proper skates. I was embarrassed after my first scrimmage that I was the only girl in figure skates, but I knew my parents weren't going to buy me hockey skates so I didn't have a choice. The second time I went out to play for the Barons, Gord McCrae lent me a pair of real hockey skates. I had to add quite a few pairs of socks onto my size-six feet so they'd fit in those size-ten boots, but I didn't care! I was playing real hockey.

In those first few games, I realized that the feeling of playing quality hockey with a rink full of other women was incredible. I think the word that best describes what I was feeling when I stepped onto that rink was *glory*. If you've ever played hockey, or another sport you truly love, I'm sure you know what I'm talking about. It's a power trip mixed with a wave of joy and self-fulfillment that wells up from the bottom of your gut and makes sparks fly through your head. I had never in my life wanted to be a part of something as badly as I wanted to play this game, and to play it the real way with referees and a scoreboard and regular linemates. Little did I know how profoundly that decision to play hockey with the Red Barons would affect my life to come.

I'll admit that beside the amazement of playing real hockey with other women, I was initially a little intimidated by the skill level and the ages of some of these ladies. Although I was only 15, the average age of the Red Barons was probably around 20 years old. Mind you, the overall variation in ages of these girls was quite substantial. We had girls of 10 playing on the same team as women old enough to be their mothers. Needless to say, the size and strength range of the team was exceedingly broad. But this diversity was necessary due to the scarcity of girls playing hockey at the time.

After a few weeks of playing with the Barons, my mother finally accepted the fact that her daughter was going to be a hockey player. She would eventually become one of my most steadfast supporters, attending nearly all of my games and tournaments. My mother was an incredible woman – a hard worker, extremely intelligent, and far ahead of her time. When she was only 15, she attended teacher's college in Ottawa. At 16, she came back to Sydenham and taught children aged 3 to 14 in a one-room schoolhouse at the corner of Rutledge Road and Division Street, an area known as Missouri. That schoolhouse had a big wood stove in the centre, around which my mother calmly sheltered her students during a tornado that narrowly missed the building.

I think this is a prime example of the courage and willpower I so admire in Mum, but the most important thing she taught me was to be responsible for my own destiny. She showed me that in life, you need to try your best to keep learning, but it is equally important for you to take your future into your own hands, go out into the world, and apply what you learn to help others grow as well. I've tried to live by this as best I could.

I'm sure my mother is responsible for much of my athleticism, although she never talked much about any sports she might have played in her youth. I suppose that is an unfortunate result of the patriarchal culture we lived in. But even in her 50s and 60s, my mother was quite agile, despite having gained a substantial amount of weight after her seven pregnancies. She was proof that size doesn't need to be a limiting factor in your confidence and capabilities. Her brilliant mind and interest in sports were certainly sources of inspiration to me in my youth.

I recall a day in my late 20s, when I took my mother and father to a Toronto Blue Jay's game, and Mum became involved in a debate with another fan over who should be chosen for the all-star team. She listed stats and interpreted skills about such and such a player so deftly that she had convinced her seatmate that he should choose her player instead of his own. I listened on in wonder at the clever arguments and incredible memory my mother had just used to change the opinion of the man beside her.

However, I regret to report that my father was rather typical of his age. I don't remember him coming to any of my games, although he didn't seem to have trouble making it out to watch my brothers play. Yet I'm sure in his own way, he played a part in my love for the sport.

Hockey was almost a ritual for us. Every Saturday night, we would all sit together and watch *Hockey Night in Canada*, and take our turns having our *weekly* baths during the intermissions and commercial breaks! We always had popcorn. If it was a good day and my Dad was in a really nice mood, he would treat us with delicious homemade caramel popcorn balls.

Things weren't always the most stable at home, due to the stressful nature of my father's job, and the difficult task my mother faced with having to raise and feed seven children while working part-time as a supply teacher. Tensions were high, but my mother did her best to keep everything peaceful. When my father came home after work, Mum would rush into the kitchen, put on her lipstick and change out of her apron just so she could look good for her husband. Sometimes, if my father had a bad day, we wouldn't talk at the dinner table – we would tap our glasses to signal to Mum that we'd like a refill so as to not disturb the silence for my father.

However, Dad's lack of interest in my sporting activity was still a step up from the discrimination girls had to put up with from some of the other members of our community. I distinctly remember being nicknamed "Ralph" by the boys at school due to my interest in hockey and other sports, along with the nickname "Beak" because I'd had a deviated septum and couldn't have surgery until my jaw finished growing at age 13. It was the ridiculousness of these nicknames that helped me realize it really didn't matter what others thought of me, so long as I was happy with myself.

In the 1960s and '70s, young women playing sports were often social misfits, and I was no exception. I never thought I fit in with most of the other girls because I didn't enjoy their games as much as I did the boys', and we didn't have many interests in common. But hockey would give me some lifelong friends, girls such as Barb Compeau, who enjoyed playing taboo sports just as much as I did. Consequently, Barb and I have remained friends for the past five decades.

Over the years, many great men and women would be added to my life along with Barb, as hockey introduced me to some of my closest friends and role models, especially during my time with the Red Barons. The power of sports in uniting a community should never be underestimated: all the more reason to ensure that *everyone* has the opportunity to be fully accepted and welcome in the game.

The Era of the Kingston Red Barons

This chapter is dedicated to the Red Barons who have since passed.

–

Judy Wilson, Helen Tucker, Betty Fowler, Deb McCaw, Claudette Grimshaw, "Pipes" Bob Weatherdon, and Eldon and Beth Aylesworth, may you rest in peace knowing that your contributions to the sport will never be forgotten.

In the 1970s, the Kingston Red Barons were not only one of the best hockey teams in the country, they were also my family.

Katherine "Cookie" Cartwright and Annabelle "Twitter" Twiddy co-founded the team after chatting at a tournament in Picton in 1968. They decided that there was no reason Kingston couldn't have a women's team like Toronto and Montreal, and decided to see if they could make that happen. This led to the creation of the ad I saw in the local paper asking for girls who were interested in forming a community team.

Cookie and Annabelle became co-captains a year later (1969), when our new team joined the Quinte Women's Hockey League, which was comprised of teams in Picton, Peterborough, Norwood, Stirling, and Belleville. Shortly thereafter, we decided to call ourselves the *Red Barons* after the well-known Peanuts character. Cookie wrote to Charles Schultz, creator of the Peanuts universe, and he wrote back and kindly gave us permission to use the famous name and a Snoopy logo for our jerseys!

It didn't take long playing with the team to realize that Cartwright and Twiddy were two of the most wonderful and powerful females I would ever meet. Although a few years my senior, they were not only my friends but also my role models. Annabelle Twiddy, a strong winger with a wicked shot, offered me sound advice about hockey both as a player with the Red Barons, and later, as the coach of the Queen's team while I was a student there (yes, I did end up playing on the team I'd aspired to in my youth!).

Annabelle was a fantastic coach, and was able to help us run excellent practices and drills with what she had learned from her playing years. Later, she would even help me out by giving me a job as a lifeguard at the YM-WCA, as she was the program director for our local branch. This, combined with the hours I spent as the only female referee for the Church Athletic League for boys' hockey, helped put me through my schooling.

Moreover, Annabelle often gave me rides to and from the rink before I had my drivers' licence. This was perhaps a more valuable service than she knew, and not only for games that I couldn't get to by bus. Annabelle was also doing me a big favour by providing an out before I could drive, on nights when my father would be asleep in his chair after a hard day at work and a few too many drinks, and my mother was too busy to give me a lift. I'm sure that in the later years I would have walked over broken glass to get to that rink, because in a way, the Red Barons unknowingly gave me the support and stability in my life that I wasn't always able to find at home.

Cookie too, was a fabulous mentor during my time with the Red Barons. Katherine Cartwright came from a family of Loyalists who settled in Kingston following the American Revolution, and she became a lawyer like both of her parents. Cookie was a fantastic hockey player. She had grown up playing with her brother at their home on the river, and in her bantam year, she tried out for a local boys' team. Tryouts were going well until her toque fell off, revealing her long hair and with it, her gender. After her disguise was revealed, Cookie was not allowed to continue with the team even though she would later prove herself one of the best women players in the country. It's a pity the boys' team didn't recognize what a valuable 11-year old asset they had just rejected.

Cookie was also one of the few girls who pushed to re-install the Queen's women's varsity team in the early 1960s, as there had been no women's team since the war. Cookie finally convinced the school administration to sanction a team after she discovered three boxes full of old hockey equipment under the stands in the old Jock Harty Arena on Arch Street, which had been wrapped in mothballs and stored there from before the war!

After this breakthrough, the school had no choice but to let the girls form a team, as their main holdout had been that it was too expensive to buy equipment for the girls, even though Cookie remembers seeing on a report from that time that the school's funding for *all* the women's sports was equal to the money allotted just for the uniform cleaning budget of the men's football team.

It was thanks to that box of ratty equipment in 1963, Cookie's third of seven years at the University, that we would see the rebirth of women's hockey at Queen's in the form of the new Queen's Golden Gals – yet another amazing institution whose very existence I owe to Katherine Cartwright.[25]

During my first years with the Barons, it was amazing to play on the ice with someone of the caliber of Cookie Cartwright, and in my later years, it was equally amazing to be coached by someone so caring and talented. Cookie was never short of jokes (she was the one to come up with my team nickname: "Honda"), and her heart was always in the right place. I remember playing for hours on end on Sunday afternoons at the beautiful Cartwright house on the St Lawrence Waterway. Cookie would somehow manage to have a rink shovelled off and flooded for us on the river, which always froze over

---

[25] Years later, the program was guided and protected by Cookie's dear friend Ann Turnbull, who worked at Queen's in Women's Athletics. Ann's shoes were later filled by my Queen's and Red Barons teammate, Janean (Gerow) Sargeant.

in those days. I don't even remember stopping for food or rest. We were thriving on hockey and fresh air.

But Cookie was more than a sports mentor for me. The Barons were a tight family, and Cookie looked out for her sisters. When I was about 19, I took a year off and worked as a teller at the Bank of Nova Scotia to try to make enough money to put myself through University and buy a car. I wasn't rich, so I knew that if I was going to go to Queen's, I would have to live at home and I would need my own vehicle to get there everyday. The hard work paid off and I was able to buy a Ford Cortina, which I named "Thelma," to help me get back and forth between school, practice and work. (Although some days, I swear it felt like my teammates and I pushed Thelma more than we drove her!)

One day, Thelma and I were in a car accident on the way to work, thanks to some stormy weather we'd had. A few days later when I got to the rink for practice, Cookie asked me how my week was, and I told her I'd been in a collision. She asked if I'd been charged and I replied that I had. Right away, Cookie told me that should never have happened because of the bad weather, and that she would challenge the charges for me. We went to court and she did exactly that, winning our case. I didn't have to pay a cent, either to the province or for her legal fees. She did it all pro bono.

Cookie also had a big Econovan with an open cab in the back. We used to throw our equipment in the rear, and then all pile in on top of it and drive to whatever tournament we were playing that weekend. It was a huge responsibility on Cookie's shoulders to cart us all around like that, but we were grateful to her for giving us a free ride! One time, we were playing in Cooper, Ontario, way out in the middle of the wilderness. The old arena there was almost archaic. Instead of using a clock and a buzzer, they kept time with a stopwatch and ended the periods by banging on a gong! I remember the rink was cold that day, there was practically no heat in the changerooms, and the only washrooms were outhouses!

When we came out after the game, it was late at night, there were very few people left at the arena, and our trusty Econovan was too cold to start. The coyotes were beginning to yip in the field behind us, and I listened on in horror as we pushed the huge van through the cold. We were all very glad when we finally got the clutch to pop and could make our way home as fast as possible!

Beside Annabelle and Cookie, there were other notable women who held ranks with the Red Barons in their inaugural years. Among the original members, we had Helen Tucker (now deceased), an engineer who would commute all the way from Ottawa, the amazing baseball player Pat Fowler (who is apparently related to me but I don't know how), her cousin Betty Fowler (now deceased), Nancy Seale, the sister of one of my brother Ed's hockey teammates, Jill Patterson, Jo-Anne Patterson, Debbie Murray, Barb Compeau, Judy Wilson, Chris Garbutt, Connie McCullough, Paula Passmore, Janet Stafford, and Joan Burns and Jean Davidson from Brockville. We even had 10-year-old Kim "Scrape" Fergusen, a tiny talented go-getter notorious for digging hard along the boards, who was the daughter of NHL player Lorne Ferguson.

But other players joined us as the team's credibility increased over the years. We later made the acquisition of Sue Reynolds, Betty Smallridge, Kathy Curtis, who later played in Brockville, the ever-entertainer Deb McCaw (now deceased), nurse Janet "Flo" Fenemore, named after Florence Nightingale, tiny Barb "Beefy" Fee, the amazing goalie Wanda "Gydie" Gyde, and star Kingston athlete Mary Skeggs.

We also had a rather timid girl by the name of Verna Lee. Every team needs a Verna Lee – Verna was like our team cheerleader, and although she was as quiet as a mouse at team functions, one could tell she was thrilled to be part of the team and her enthusiasm was endearing. The Red Barons also obtained players who came to us via the Queen's program, such as Karen Sculley. Karen must have been 5'10" but we called her "Tiny!" Furthermore, many of Kingston's finest ball players made the transition to become hockey players, like Faye Tracey, who played wing with me and our centre Cookie.

These were but a few of the incredible women I played with, although there were certainly more to wear the Red Baron sweater in the years after I left.

By the 1973-74 season, our pool of talented young women had helped the Red Barons move out of the Quinte League and up to the Senior A level. Due to the distances between the women's A teams (which consisted of ladies from Toronto, Montreal, and Kingston), it would have been difficult to form a regular league, so we were restricted to tournaments and exhibition games in order to play competitive hockey.

It was in this period that the Red Barons made the acquisition of Carol Pettey, a strong young woman who came from a big corn farm in Campbellford, Ontario. Carol actually rented the top room in my house during our university years. I remember we would get up at 5:30 for early morning practices and put our equipment on in the basement of the house, rather than have to change in the freezing cold arena! There we were, in full equipment except for our skates and helmet, driving in Thelma to a 6 am practice on a weekday! Quite the sight, I'm sure!

Carol was one of my best friends all through university, and we had some great times together. The girl was really unique, so we decided to call her Carol *Quincey* Pettey, to make her initials sound distinguished when we wrote letters to her. We decided that nothing was more aristocratic that the letter *Q*, and that *Quincey* was a nice name for the *Q* to stand for, and so, she was henceforth known as *Quincey* to the Red Barons.

We had what we called the "breakfast club" for the Queen's and Red Baron's players, where we took turns going to teammates' houses for breakfast after practices. I remember one 6 am practice on November 11, 1975, where I managed to catch the puck from a deflected slap shot with my face, and absolutely shattered my nose. I had to be driven to the hospital by Quincey. The blood covering my face was so bad that the doctor mistook me for a boy! ("Put *him* over there," he said).

When we came back from the hospital after practice, everyone was up in Carol's room, since it was her day to serve breakfast from the mini-kitchenette in her loft apartment above our house. Somehow she still managed to have breakfast prepared and ready for the gang, even though she had taken me to the hospital!

The team was lucky enough to acquire Janean "G" Gerow around the same time as Carol. Janean came from a good hockey family. She was the daughter of the well-known Napanee OHA coach Walt Gerow, and she had the most wicked slapshot I've ever seen in a woman's league. Quincey and G were both amazing players and could easily have made a provincial team if they'd had the chance.

The Barons would also benefit then from the skills of Sue Scherer, the rough and tough daughter of the Kingston Canadian's General Manager Walter "Punch" Scherer. Sue Scherer would become our Captain in her later years, and would go on to coach women's hockey at the international level. She would even come out of retirement (a.k.a. coaching) to play as Captain for Team Canada at the World Championships in the early 1990s, before returning to coach Cassie Campbell on the Guelph University team a few years later.

All three girls would prove to be some of the best players in the Barons' history, and in the case of Sue Scherer, in the whole of women's hockey history.

We also acquired a girl by the name of Sue Wright, a player from a team in Stirling, Ontario, another one of the top girls on our team. Sue Wright, in my opinion, was a better hockey player even than Scherer, and hockey legend Dave McMaster once told Cookie that Sue was one of only three perfect skaters he had ever met, the other two being Paul Coffey and Bobby Orr.

Wright never went on to play at the national level, although certainly not for lack of ability. I think it is very possible that Sue Wright was one of the best female hockey players of all time. Sadly, Sue accepted a job after graduating from Queen's just at the time the national team started training out in Calgary, and so ended her career in hockey.

It is unfortunate that the world will never know the talent of athletes as incredible as Sue Wright, mainly due to the lack of media attention available for women playing high level hockey. I am bitter at the thought that the lack of financial support for female hockey players has hindered so many girls like Sue from becoming full-time athletes. Who knows how many possible stars have been lost due to the lack of funding for female players at the higher levels?

Women in hockey today are facing the same problems. Elite athletes who have the opportunity to focus on their sport full-time are able to advance so much farther in their training, especially compared to those who have to work a 40-hour week at a fast food restaurant just to make a living. Think of what these women might be able to accomplish if they were given the chance to devote their lives to a sport like the men can. It angers me greatly to think that many professional male hockey players in North America make more, alone, than the total financial support received by all of the professional female players in the CWHL and the NWHL combined.26

Despite the flagrant disparity that persists today, professional women's hockey has made considerable headway since the 1970s, when ragamuffin teams like the Red Barons were the most that women in the sport could aspire to. We were even named the "champions" of North America in 1975-76, at a tournament in Wallaceburg, Ontario called the Wallaceburg *Lipstick* Tournament.27

However, I believe the term "widely regarded as" is a better substitute to being "officially recognized as" the national champions, as the infrastructure required to claim something to that extent wouldn't be available for girls in hockey until the 1980s and 90s. We certainly didn't look like professionals, and none of us had any kind of salaries or bursaries. Gosh, we would have been hard pressed to find a girl who didn't have any holes in her equipment!28

Appearances aside, the quality of our hockey was nonetheless some of the best in North America at the time. We Barons added to our reputation by beating internationally-renowned teams like the Boston Massport Jets. By the winter of 1974-75, the Jets had been

26 Compare the $3.7 million per year allotted for the entire budget of the Canadian Women's Hockey League (which recently folded due to lack of funding), to the $15.9 million doled out this year to John Tavares by the Toronto Maple Leafs.

27 I'm sure this name would never be accepted today, but back then many were trying to feminize the sport by associating it with traditional "girly" symbolism in order to increase public approval.

28 As a prime example of this dishevelment, Annabelle even had a duct-tape "X" on the butt of her hockey pants, and we used to joke that it was a target when she was in front of the net!

undefeated for 95 games in a row until their encounter with the Red Barons.

If ever there was a well-funded "professional-like" hockey team back then, it was the Massport Jets. Formed in 1970 by youth hockey advocate and coach Anthony Marmo, the Jets were partially-sponsored by the Massachusets Transportation Authority, which was also the inspiration for their name.[29] Thanks to this financial support, the players had brand-new matching equipment, and travelled in a coach bus.

Prior to their arrival, the Massport Jets sent a pamphlet detailing their history and reputation to warn us exactly what a quality team we were up against! The warning was certainly well-deserved, although not in the way they intended.

In those days we played full-contact hockey, and our game against the Jets was no exception. It was rough to begin with, but when the American team realized they weren't going to win, they started making dirty hits left, right and centre, not unlike the Philadelphia Broad Street Boys of the 1970s. By the end of the game, a handful of girls had dropped their gloves and we had a full-on brawl. To this day, this is the only real fight I have ever witnessed in a women's hockey game. I remember someone picked up little 10-year-

[29]Massport Jets Records. Schlesinger Library, Radcliffe Institute. Harvard Library, https://hollis.harvard.edu/primo-explore/fulldisplay?docid=01HVD_ALMA212032117760003941&context=L&vid=HVH2&lang=en_US&search_scope=everything&adaptor=Local%20Search%20Engine&tab=everything&query=any,contains,massport%20jets&offset=0. Accessed 15 Oct. 2019.

old Fergie and placed her behind the bench for safety, and I went right along and sat beside her to avoid the fight myself!

Yet the Jets weren't the only violent team we had to face, and I'm sure the women's program has had a few other fisticuffs since. Contrary to popular belief, women aren't actually made of sugar and spice but rather of muscles and personality, making us at times just as, if not more competitive than men.

Despite this occasional violence, I had a lot of fun during my eight seasons with the Barons. I remember we would have intense baby powder wars in the changeroom before games, and sometimes a player would be so saturated with the stuff that a white mushroom cloud would puff out from under their equipment when they took a hit during the game. I think I should have bought stock shares in Johnson and Johnson, because we went through so much of that stuff I'd have been rich.

We had all kinds of jokes with the team. We used to do "red-light fire drills" to practice our speed and agility on our way to games. When we stopped, everyone would jump out, run around the car, and hop back in before the light turned green and the vehicle started moving again. The people behind us must have thought we were crazy!

Another time, one of our players, Deb McCaw, was pretending to walk out of the door buck naked. Well, the laughs were on her when our coach chose that exact moment to open the door, and caught her as bare the day she was born! It hit the team hard in our later years when Deb and one of her sons were killed in a car crash after hitting a patch of black ice in Prince Edward County.

I can remember Deb wearing a beautiful black dress and dangling pewter earrings made out of an old fork and spoon – we used to tease her that whenever we went on road trips, she brought her own cutlery! I can write about Deb's humour and the change room incident without shame, because she was so open-minded and was never embarrassed by anything – she laughed at these jokes as much as we did! Though I suppose that was one problem with having male coaches for a female team, and yet another reason among many for women to be given the chance to coach at higher levels.

Mind you, even though most of the coaches in our early years were male, they were still fantastic people and all dedicated supporters of our women's hockey movement. Our first coach was Ron Passmore, followed shortly after by Geoff Hoyle, who was Cookie Cartwright's boyfriend at the time.

Geoff was a really lovely individual, but couldn't skate for the life of him! Geoff didn't really know much about hockey, but he was learning quickly! He ran all our practices from the sidelines, which was not an ideal coaching situation, but we didn't hold it against him because we were living in the era of innovators such as Viktor Tikhonov, a Russian National coach who won three Olympic golds and eight world championships, and helped make the Soviets the most dominant team in the world.30 And even if Geoff lacked Tikhonov's incredible coaching ability, he was really good at opening the bench doors, so I suppose that was a start!

We had a lot of trouble finding coaches who would stay in the program after Geoff, mostly due to the lack of financial compensation available as well as the public's general lack of tolerance for women in the sport. But we did have one coach who wasn't opposed to facing this kind of adversity, and who supported us through multiple seasons. His name was Bob Weatherdon.

Bob truly dedicated a part of his life to our team. He would chip in from his own pocket to travel with us to all our games and tournaments, and he was present at every 6 and 7 am practice (we practiced so early because it was so difficult to get icetime back then, and especially for a women's team). He was the manager at the local Loblaws, and if any of our players needed a job, Bob took care of them. He had us collect coupons so that he could take them into work and exchange them for cash to help us pay for our icetime.

We were also well received by his wife Nancy, who became the "team mom." Their kids Janet and Kirk would help carry our equipment and cheer us on from the stands. The Weatherdons' were even kind enough to invite us into their home for visits, helping to foster the Red Baron family. They genuinely cared about women's

---

30 The Associated Press. "Viktor Tikhonov, legendary Soviet Union hockey coach, dead at 84." *CBC Sports*, 24 Nov. 2014, www.cbc.ca/sports/hockey/nhl/viktor-tikhonov-legendary-soviet-union-hockey-coach-dead-at-84-1.2846640. Accessed 16 July 2019.

hockey. We still keep in touch with Nancy today, although, sadly, Bob has passed away.

Over the years, as our program grew and became better known to the public, it began to gain more support from the community. The Red Barons were lucky enough to have had two referees who treated us with the utmost respect. Whenever we could afford them, we would hire Phil Marshal or/and Dave Descent to officiate our games because they took us seriously, unlike the majority of other referees we could find, who usually lollygagged and called our games as if we were a bunch of kids playing pond hockey.

Thanks to these two individuals, the women's hockey world of the '70s enjoyed playing against the Red Barons, because Phil and Dave made sure the game was called according to CAHA (Canadian Amateur Hockey Association) rules and helped us achieve the authenticity we sought.

As our respectability began to blossom, greater opportunities for the advancement of the women's hockey program in Kingston came into existence. After my first season, I had the opportunity to attend one of the first hockey schools for female players, which was held at the local Kingston Memorial Community Centre, organized by arena manager Ron Clark and some other "hockey people" from around the city.

The facilitators provided discounts for people who hosted girls from out of town at their home for the week of the camp. I was somehow able to convince my mother to let us host three billets that year, meaning I was able to attend the camp for free![31] One of the billets was centre Cathy Brown from Toronto, who later became one of my face-off opponents when I started playing with the Golden Gals in the University circuit.

It was at this camp that I learned to raise the puck and was able to improve a lot of my other skills as well. I'd also just bought my first pair of Tacks – brand new hockey skates. However, I had naively forgotten to sharpen the blades before trying them out, which resulted in a pulled groin only a few hours into the camp! I was humiliated! There was absolutely no way that I was going to admit to our first aid respondent, fourth-year medical student Dave Fields, the reason I was limping so badly for the rest of the week!

Later, in the 1973-74 season, the Barons would partner with the Kingston Lion's Club and the Kingston Township Recreation Department to organize the "Red Barons' House League," a farm system to introduce young girls and new players of older ages to the wonderful sport of women's hockey. The house league provided an opportunity for 3 or 4 teams' worth of players (about 50-odd girls) to get active, work on their hockey skills, and of course, to have fun.

The Barons would profit from this farm system early on by the addition of players like 5'7" Carolyn "Shorty" Aylesworth, who at 13 was already talented enough to move up the ranks to the Senior A Barons. With Carolyn came "Shorty's dad," Eldon Aylesworth, our

[31] The billeting involved hosting or being hosted at the house of another person for a certain amount of time, and living with the stranger as with family. It helped to cut down on costs for all parties involved, which was especially useful for programs such as girls' hockey where parents were less likely to spend money for hotel stays.

team manager, who was another strong male supporter, not only for his daughter, but for our whole team. Men like Bob and Eldon were so important to the women's movement, because convincing girls that they're as worthy and capable as men is only half the battle.

With the help of these supporters, the Barons organized a tournament in 1973 which drew girls from all over Ontario and Québec. Our major food at this event was provided by my brother-in-law, Al Mariotti, who worked for Corsh at the time. He was kind enough to give us all the corned beef that was about to expire in a few days, and with the help of my mother, we sold corned beef on rye to cover the tournament's expenses. We never had much money, so we had to fundraise in all the creative ways we could. Thankfully, this tournament turned out to be a success, and along with the house league system, it really helped to increase the popularity and acceptance of girls' hockey in Kingston at the time.

On top of running programs to support the development of women's hockey, the Red Barons were also involved in a few camps and workshops to promote the similar sport of Ringette. Invented by Sam Jacks, ringette was considered the "girl's version" of hockey, and is played with a rubber ring, a straight stick, has different rules than the "men's sport," and different feminized age categories as well: *Petites, Tweens, Belles, Juniors,* and *Debutants.*[32]

Jacks, Director of Parks and Recreation for North Bay at the time of ringette's conception, designed the game specifically for

[32] Etue and Williams, *On the Edge,* p. 44-50.

women and proceeded to push it out to the Society of Directors of Municipal Recreation of Ontario.33 The society readily took up Jacks' idea and began funding programs for girls in the sport in the next few years as a non-violent and "feminine" alternative to hockey. By 1969, the Ontario Ringette Association had been formed, and registration numbers would grow to as much as 20,000 girls playing in Canada by 1985.34

Peter Lawson, from the Kingston Recreation Department, hired the Red Barons in 1974 to host ringette clinics and training sessions throughout the city in exchange for icetime for the Red Barons. I always harboured the feeling that maybe the Rec Department was trying to make a few more ringette players out of our team, not to mention making the same of the young girls who attended our camps.

However, girls' hockey was growing rapidly on its own, despite government interest in the rival sport of ringette, because the push for hockey came from the grassroots-level up as opposed to downward from the top of the hierarchy. I remember attending the annual Easter Hockey Tournament hosted by the Brampton Canadettes, which quickly became an Easter weekend tradition I enjoyed even more than egg hunts. In my first year, I believe the tournament had about 27 teams. But by my eighth season, I would

33 "History of Ringette." *Ringette Canada,* www.ringette.ca/our-sport/history-of-ringette/. Accessed 28 May 2019.
34 Ibid.

wager that number had expanded more than threefold, and no thanks to governmental support.

Despite this grassroots-level growth, hockey was still not universally accepted as a legitimate sport for girls. In fact, many made a mockery of our involvement in the sport. I recall one time the Red Barons were offered the chance to gain some positive exposure by playing a short scrimmage against a few members of the local media (all male), during the intermission of a Kingston Aces' Senior A men's game. We were really excited to get such a high-profile opportunity to showcase our talent and prove what women in hockey were capable of achieving.

Unfortunately, our opponents seemed to think that this game was nothing more than a ridiculous farce. During the match, I remember one man was in the corner, clowning around like he didn't know how to play the sport. I was so mad, I grabbed the puck and ripped it around the boards behind him, and I think he grumbled something along the lines of, "Oh, you girls really take your hockey serious!" He thought we wouldn't know what we were doing, and that it was just meant to be a ham of a game.

Even through this lack of social acceptance, I thoroughly enjoyed my time with the Barons. They were a fundamental part of my growth as a young girl, a constant source of inspiration and support. The Barons helped me realize what a fantastic support network organized sports can provide for young girls. Not only are these teams a source of fun, but they also give us lasting connections, and teach us invaluable life skills like perseverance and collaboration.

Playing with the Red Barons taught me so much that I could never have learned at University, but that was so important later on in the corporate world.

Playing with the Queen's Golden Gals

While the Red Barons will always hold a special place in my heart, it is also worth remembering my time with the Queen's Golden Gals,[35] as they too had a major formative role in my youth.

I played three seasons with the Golden Gals, from 1973 to 1976. We practiced three days a week in the beautiful new Jock Harty Arena, and we had our games on the weekends. Along with Cookie and Annabelle, who were both coaches at Queen's during my years of play, there were many overlapping players between the Barons, the Barons' House League, and the Golden Gals, who served to reinforce the community of women hockey players that was beginning to grow in our town.

---

[35] The Queen's women's teams were commonly known as the "Golden Gals" in the 60s and 70s to differentiate ourselves from the men's teams. However, the Queen's women's teams would transition to be known as the "Golden Gaels" in the 1980s (which had technically been our name all along, although we were never known by it, since it was the name our male counterparts sported); Flegg, Erin. "Final days of a hockey legacy," *The Queen's Journal,* 5 Apr. 2007, https://www.queensjournal.ca/story/2007-04-05/news/final-days-hockey-legacy/. Accessed 16 Sept. 2019;

The skill level of the Red Barons was far superior to that of the Golden Gals thanks to the wider area and age range the Barons could draw from, but it sure felt more like professional hockey to play with a university team compared to the tatterdemalion Barons. In contrast, the Queen's team was exceedingly well funded (or should I say, it was funded). We were given matching equipment and uniforms, we had our own dressing room, we travelled on a really nice Greyhound bus, we stayed in superb hotels for distant games and tournaments, and we had a meal allowance! The Golden Gals even had their own trainer, which was especially handy for me because I broke my collarbone so many times that it became a chronic nuisance during my competitive years.

The media visibility for Queen's was another factor that contributed to the perception that we were playing high-level hockey. We had our pictures taken and many of our games were covered in the campus newspapers. And this was even during an era when it unheard of for girls' teams like the Barons to make the headlines, with the exception, of course, of articles that attempted to prove that women's hockey even existed.

All in all, the exposure and paid expenses made this kind of treatment seem like the best a woman hockey player could ask for in those days. We felt like elite-level athletes in the closest thing to a professional league that we could get.

I believe the men's program received proportionally equal funding to us, although they had many more games and tournaments to play in since there were more varsity men's teams available as opponents. The only varsity women's teams we had were McMaster, Guelph (coached by powerhouse Shirley Peterson), Western, York University, and the University of Toronto (coached by women's hockey legend Dave McMaster, who was also the dedicated coach of the first Canadian Women's National Team). We only had these six since our program was just beginning to resurface after its lull during the war. Consequently, the boys may have been given more travel and expense money overall, but as a whole, the equality of the financial disbursement was fair.

Mind you, in my first year playing at Queen's, the ice times given out were pretty discriminatory. The boys' team always got the prime ice, with practices right after school, around 5 pm. The girls had to go home and come back later, around 6:30 or 7:00 pm, and our games were always on Friday and Saturday nights when most of the other college students would be out partying.

Thankfully, by the time I graduated, the administration had finally come to see the folly in their ways and the boys had to alternate the days they got to play and practice during prime icetime in order to share it with us women. Ann Turnbull was a great help here again, as she was always lobbying for resources for the girls' team at Queen's.

In terms of equality today, one aspect the administration is still missing is in the recognition of their past athletes. At Queen's, the boys' hockey team has their own Hall of Fame to honour previous superstars, but there is still no Hall of Fame for the women's team! This fact could reflect an unfortunate lopsidedness in the donations coming from our Alumni. Many of my old teammates and I still give to the Queen's program, as our group is one of the few who understand first-hand the importance of the system, but sadly, there are not many groups after us who share the same mentality.

And although the administration was pretty fair with us in our day, the male players either ignored us, or were disgruntled that we were taking away from "their" resources. A lot of the men didn't support the culture shift that was occurring and putting more women in sport. Some still felt that it simply wasn't "right" that girls played hockey too, or that if we did, it must be no more than some kind of entertaining joke like it had been when the Red Barons were humiliated by the mockery from our adversaries in the scrimmage against our local media.

It was so annoying to never be taken seriously. I loved the game and I played just as much as the varsity men, but it was never as impressive when I got up at 5:30 am to sweat out a hard practice compared to when a man did the exact same thing. A few parents, and to some extent, female players, claimed that women's hockey was naturally less intense than the men's, and reasoned that girls were innately less competitive than boys. I believe, however, that the true logic behind this lack of "intensity" (otherwise known as fights and screaming parents), was that up until the 1990s, women were perfectly aware that they were never going to make a career out of the game like men and we adjusted our level of "seriousness" accordingly. But that didn't mean that we didn't want to win a fair game of competitive hockey! We just weren't going to cry about it if we didn't.

On top of the exclusion and mockery, there was some derogatory "offside" teasing that occurred, which certainly didn't help our self-esteem and certainly didn't help increase the acceptance of girls in sport. In hindsight, this kind of teasing is an interesting paradox. Although now it is so easy to see the discrimination that lay behind all those jokes and comments, many of them never bothered us at the time they happened. In fact, some of them seemed downright funny!

I remember eating dinner with the team during one of our Queen's road trip dinners and joking with the waiter about the life of women hockey players. We somehow got into a discussion about hockey players missing teeth, prompting him to start singing "All I Want for Christmas is my Two Front Teeth." Little did he know that I'd been in a biking accident in grade seven and had lost the bottom half of both my front teeth, which had been replaced with a partial plate. Well, when he came back to give us our food, I had removed my plate and gave him a great big gaping smile. He was so sorry that he'd been teasing us about our looks and apologized profusely. We, however, thought the whole situation was quite comical. [36]

But some of the jokes we were involved in weren't quite as good-natured, although we continued to laugh at them for the sake of maintaining face. One joke that still sticks in my mind today is the

[36] See appendix A for a drawing by Cookie of me as a character from the Peanut's universe, making fun of hockey players with missing teeth.

derogatory line that a lot of the guys would often ask me in teasing after a game: *"did you score any goals?"* But what they meant was: *"did you *... any women?* "This was exactly the kind of macho male culture that drove us half mad.

And there were other jokes that somehow stuck with me throughout the years, like being called "Ralph." That horrible nickname might as well have been sewn into the back of my jersey from the time I was 13 until I was 23. I even remember coming home to Kingston as a full-grown woman, 46 years old, and being astonished when a business acquaintance called me by that same name, which they must have picked up from someone in town! But even though this nickname stung, I would never have thought of complaining about it. I assumed it was just part of the culture.

The fact that we weren't offended by these kinds of jokes – and believe me, they were often far worse- only serves to prove the extent to which we had all been brainwashed by our patriarchal society. Even if we knew first-hand how frustrating it was to be seen as second-class citizens, and that it was just plain wrong for women to be denied access to sports and other "men's" domains purely on the basis of gender, we still failed to critically assess a lot of the hard words that were thrown at us. We were too caught up in the collective fictions that society had been feeding to us since birth to be able to see the extent to which those doctrines were deep-rooted within us. Even though we were ardently promoting equality for women, we were still unknowingly perpetuating male domination by laughing at those stupid sexist jokes.

It's been quite some time since I last set foot in a university locker room, but I sincerely hope that those kinds of "jokes" aren't weighing on the subconscious of young women in sport today. But if they are, I hope that these girls can at least find the nerve to get up and laugh right back at the ridiculous patriarchal culture from which they emanate, because that is the real joke here.

In the end, as female athletes, we learned to fend for ourselves, with or without the encouragement of our peers and parents. I found support in my fellow teammates, and together, we managed to win the OWIAA (Ontario Women's Intercollegiate Athletic Association) title in the 1974-75 season, my second year of university. I discovered early that we didn't need any feedback or positive reinforcement from others to succeed. We could move forward on our own.

Battling Stereotypes

"Who says girls can't play hockey?
Girls can play hockey as good as the boys, so why
shouldn't we?
Who said it was just for boys?
Boys, that's who."

-Vicki Westervelt, 11, goalie.[37]

Let me tell you a little bit more about the false assumptions a lot of the "jokes" were based upon, starting off with the idea that rough sports like hockey had the innate ability to "masculinize" all the women who played them.

It never fails to astound me just how far gender-role stereotypes could infiltrate all aspects of our lives back in my youth. They affected the way women worked, dressed, walked, talked, the hobbies we took up, the values we followed, and of course, the sports we played. Women were expected to be passive, dainty, delicate, and

---

[37] Quoted in Brown, Susan. "Slapshot! It's their turn on the ice," *Detroit Free Press* [Detroit], 1 Feb. 1982.

the choices of "women's sports" available to us reflected these characteristics.

Figure skating, tennis, rhythmic gymnastics – these were the activities "ladies" were supposed to play, *if* we chose to be involved in sports at all. But for the few of us who broke the mould and decided to try our hand at lacrosse, soccer, rugby, hockey, etc., we were apparently physically and psychologically transformed by these games.

Growing up, it was expected that if we played these "men's' sports," we would lose our status as "true women" by bulking up with "unsightly" muscles, becoming aggressive, more competitive, more successful, and overall more "manly." This idea was perhaps not entirely untrue, because sports usually helped to increase the fitness and successfulness of any individual, whatever their sex or gender. But the idea that these traits were fundamentally *masculine* is where the theory lost its validity. I was by no means less a woman for having muscles, playing hockey, and wanting to be successful.

To me, the most interesting part of this gender-role issue was the way in which it was propagated. The media, I believe, was the main factor responsible for these societal divisions. Newspapers and magazines, television and radio, posters, advertisements, and school curricula all tried to instill these "values" in us, but I never heard anyone tell me in person that I would become more masculine for playing hockey. Of course, many parents and a lot of our male peers were caught up in the propaganda, but as the new generation of audacious young women, we attributed little importance to what we knew were ridiculous outdated principles.

Mind you, there was a great number of instances when individuals tried to counteract the idea that sports like hockey reduced the femininity of its female athletes, again by using different media tactics to sway the public viewpoint. Of the proliferation of news articles about girl's hockey since the early 1900s, numerous stories have contained quotes from women who emphasize the fact that they wear make-up while playing or that they are "women first and hockey players second," in an attempt to convince the population that they could be every bit of the gentlewoman idealized in society at that time and still be a fantastic hockey player.[38]

This tradition of the "feminization" of the sport would continue well into the later years of the 20th Century. Besides the Wallaceburg *Lipstick* tournament already mentioned, an excellent example occurred during the organization of the first Women's Nationals in 1982. The main advertising posters that year featured the face of a beautiful woman playing hockey without her facemask (see appendix B), which was a mandatory piece of equipment according to the Canadian Amateur Hockey Association (CAHA) rules she was supposed to be playing by.

We had some difficulty working with the poster's artists leading up to the first Women's Nationals. Our sponsors wanted to try

---

[38] Bolender, Keith. "Girls' hockey? They're proving the game can be played just for fun," *The Toronto Star* [Toronto], 7 Oct. 1980; McFarlane, *Proud Past, Bright Future*, p. 81-82, 194.

and make a woman who was entirely covered in bulky hockey equipment appear "attractive" as a marketing tool. The corporate artists wanted to remove the facemasks for all the girls on the poster, to try and make their faces look alluring in order to compensate for the lack of sexualization that could be achieved in their equipment-covered bodies.

As organizers of the Championship, we argued that this facemask-less representation was an unsafe and inaccurate depiction of the game, and gave young women the wrong idea about what really mattered in the sport. In the end, we had to compromise with our sponsors, and the pretty maskless woman in the foreground was used to "feminize" the game, while the women in the background represented a more accurate picture of what I consider to be the most beautiful part of the game: the play.

This kind of feminine sexualization of women in hockey was unfortunately carried on to some extent even in the '90s. During the first Women's World Championship in March of 1990, Sport Canada decided it would be a good idea to dress our women's team in all-pink equipment and jerseys, despite protests from many of the players. Feminization like this was supposed to help increase the popularity and social acceptance of girls playing a "man's sport" like hockey, and granted, it may have in fact helped to achieve this goal. Nevertheless, it is important to recognize that these media ploys were still playing into the division created by gender-role stereotypes because they pushed the idea that a woman had to be feminine, dainty, and "pretty in pink" in order to even be considered a "woman."

Sadly, there was more behind these absurd media schemes. On top of the notion that these sports "*de*-feminized" their athletes, there were many people who believed that if women playing sports weren't "masculinized" by the game, then they must have been more "manly" to begin with. It was naturally assumed that the women who played "unfeminine" sports had some internal hormone defect which caused them to enjoy aggression and violence like men supposedly did. This, apparently, meant that we must necessarily also enjoy the company of women, like men did. It was therefore widely assumed that the majority of women athletes in "men's sports" must be lesbians, a theory built on yet another preposterous fallacy as it presupposed that lesbians are naturally "manlier" than heterosexual women!

These asinine stereotypes were something I faced personally during my years on the ice. Many individuals, my own nephew included, assumed that I was lesbian simply because I played hockey and wasn't involved in a romantic relationship during university. It would never have occurred to some people that women enjoyed playing hockey because *we liked hockey*, not because we liked violence, were lesbian, or wanted to be men.

This stigma would even follow me into corporate boardrooms as an adult, as many people couldn't seem to wrap their minds around the idea that women might also be interested in pursuing a full-time career. There was even a scientific study done by Matina Horner in

1968,[39] only one year before my hockey debut, that attempted to prove that the reason women didn't usually pursue careers was because we had a "natural fear of success." This theory was subsequently adopted by many bigots and used as an excuse to "explain" why women were never represented at the higher levels in professional sports, prestigious careers, and other structures dominated by men.

But the boundaries between men's public domains and women's private spheres were all too well defined for many, even before the Horner study, and these divisions had certainly not formed due to an "innate womanly fear" of moving up in the world. The only way to get around such culturally-imposed boundaries, of course, was to join a small group of lucky individuals who didn't care whether or not they crossed society's precious lines.

A large portion of this lucky group was comprised of young women who self-identified as "tomboys." For our purposes, let a *tomboy* be defined as a girl who doesn't blindly follow social customs, but instead, runs, jumps, throws, skates, and marches to the beat of her own drumming heart. Tomboys are free, wild, adventurous, and squeeze as much excitement out of life as they can. If they don't want to wear a skirt, they won't. If they don't want to

[39] Horner, Matina. *Sex Differences in Achievement Motivation and Performance in Competitive and Non-Competitive Situations.* Ph.D. Dissertation, University of Michigan, 1968.

wear a shirt, they don't. If they don't want to play house, they'll play hockey.

The word *tomboy* carried a certain significance, which for many, such as journalist Caryl Rivers,[40] had a physical connotation, something that denoted a transgression of "turf" boundaries. Tomboys didn't stay on their side of the gender role fence. As Caryl pointed out, some girls were proud of this name, but others had crossed to greener pastures without meaning to, so depending on who you were addressing with it, the term could earn you a smile of pride or a hearty kick to the shins.

I recall having a conversation with one of my brother's childhood friends a few years ago, and as we reminisced, he happened to mention that he thought I had been "such a tomboy" in my youth. As an adult, I was above kicking a man in the shins, which was lucky for my companion because I can't say that I found this term to be a compliment. "Tomboy" was one of those names that you could write in marker on your face with pride, but that still stung a little when someone else called you by it because the word could be loaded with so much negative energy. Tomboys weren't normal. They didn't fit in.

My friends and I wore hockey jackets and tracksuits when we hung around, as much for their comfort as for our lack of interest in mainstream fashion. I believe this physical manifestation of our

---

[40] See her article "The Girls of Summer: All the Dirt on the American Tomboy or Why Girls Say To Heck with the Prince- I'll Keep the Frog," in *womenSports,* 1977. It's absolutely fabulous.

involvement in a sport was the main reason we were considered "tomboys." As teens, none of us chewed tobacco or rolled in the mud, I can assure you, and yet we were more or less social outcasts. I remember my guidance counsellor at the Kingston Collegiate Vocational Institute, Mr. Hudson, even suggested once that I should join the Armed Forces so that I could "learn to conform" to the mould of the female idealized in society at the time.

I believe that ignoring Mr. Hudson's advice was one of the best things I did to advance my future career. Just as tomboys encroached on male "turf" in arenas and sports fields, they tended to also infringe upon men's "turf" in the business and professional worlds later on in life. It was exactly this gutsy pluck that helped me and other "tomboys" to disregard social customs and take the futures of our employment into our own hands, just as my mother had taught me.

Mum was adamant that none of her daughters would take keyboarding classes, out of fear that we would become stenotypes! She wanted us to aspire to more than secretary work if that was what we desired, and pushed us to find careers for ourselves that were equally as substantial as those of our brothers.

The determination and perseverance I learned on the ice would benefit me when I entered the business world after my interval in hockey administration, as I had already learned to critically evaluate situations, take risks when necessary, put my best effort into projects, and work well in a team. I truly believe playing hockey had a direct impact on the overall success of my career as an adult.

Hockey gave me the experience and strength I needed to walk the high wire and find a sturdy foothold for a young woman in an old man's world.

Sport contributed to our physical strength as much as our mental fortitude, as we had to learn to maintain our resiliency against the absolute falsehoods that society was spreading about female athletes. One myth that really got under my skin was the idea that girls who played sports were more prone to injury than their male counterparts. This idea expressly contradicts the notion that tomboys who played sports were more "manly," whether this was due to nature or nurture, because sport supposedly made us lose the very feminine "weakness" that would have been responsible for our increased susceptibility to injuries.

In my youth, this stereotype might have been legitimate, but only because the majority of women were physically inactive, meaning they had never developed the musculature required to protect themselves from pulling tendons, rolling their ankles, or absorbing any amount of shock. But the fact that books produced on women in sport even in the 1980s[41] had to scientifically disprove the widely-believed myth that women hit in the chest with balls and pucks were likely to develop breast cancer, shows clearly how deep this illusion of feminine weakness had been anchored into our society.

---

[41] See Hall, M. Ann, and Dorothy A. Richardson. *Fair Ball: Towards Sex Equality in Canadian Sport.* Ottawa, Canadian Advisory Council on the Status of Women, 1982, p. 79-81.

However, more modern studies, such as one done by Almeida et al. as early as 1999, show that women now have the same injury rates as men, but that the "higher injury rates often found in female[s] may be explained by gender differences in symptom reporting." [42] In other words, women themselves *thought* that they were weaker than men, so they more often disclosed their injuries to healthcare professionals, whereas men generally abstained from announcing their injuries because they had been culturally instructed that to do so was a sign of weakness. However, when women are given the chance to develop their musculature enough to adequately support their bodyweight, they become just as resistant to injuries as men. Likewise, if men do not make an effort to build up enough strength to protect themselves, they become just as prone to injuries as the women of my youth.

Another stereotype to plague most females in the 1970s was that we were considered to be more "delicate" than men because of the blood we lost during menstruation. While my school peers and I never ever shared with anyone that we were on our period, you wouldn't believe how many gym classes girls could get out of by using the excuse that they were not up to such and such a task that day. On the other side, this was not only a self-imposed barrier, but also one imposed by the patriarchally-constructed fallacy that intense sports could cause severe reproductive deficiencies in women.

[42] Almeida SA, et al. "Gender Differences in Musculoskeletal Injury Rates: A Function of Symptom Reporting?" *Medicine and Science in Sports and Exercise*, vol. 31, no. 12, 1999, p. 1807-1812.

While it is true that many women in sports suffer from amenorrhea (lack of menses) and anemia (iron deficiency sometimes related to menstruation), these conditions are usually linked to an insufficient dietary intake compared to energy output in physical exercise. Thus, these conditions are more often found in women in sports that stress thinness, such as ballet dancing or distance running. Here again, the culture surrounding the sport has had a more profound effect on the athletes than the sport itself, because with the right nutrition planning, it is very easy for a woman to eat enough to be entirely healthy and still participate in her sport at an elite level.

I am relieved that as time progressed, more and more of these stereotypes about women hockey players were dispelled. The first Women's Nationals and the first World Championship were major turning points in the level of respect society allotted to female athletes. Women in sports were increasingly being seen as the normal, even extraordinary women that they were. On a more personal note, I felt a substantial reduction in the stigma I faced from my friends and family after I started playing hockey with Queen's University, and the cynics became more convinced of our reputability after seeing a public institution treating us as serious, competent and presentable athletes. It is amazing what incredible feats just a little bit of media can accomplish.

VI

The Formation of the
Ontario Women's Hockey Association

After graduating with my B.A. from Queen's, I started looking for a job. The year was 1976 and I was 23 years old. There didn't seem to be a lot of jobs available for young people in non-metropolitan Ontario at that time, so I couldn't afford to be picky. Out of sheer luck, I spotted an ad in *The Toronto Star* for the position of aquatics coordinator for the Board of Education in the remote town of Kapuskasing, situated 1,000 kilometres north-west of Kingston, just a few hours past Timmins. I replied to the ad and submitted my resume by mail, and a few weeks later on a cold October day, I took my mother and we drove 11 hours north through the wilderness to interview for the job in person.

I remember we stopped about halfway through our trip because there had been some snow and our car had got a flat. We were lucky enough to have hit a stretch of road that was probably a good 50 miles of pure boonies with no towns or hamlets to speak of, somewhere between Smooth Rock Falls and Cochrane. This was probably one of the most desolate sections of the Trans-Canada highway in Northern Ontario, and we didn't have a phone or any way of contacting an emergency mechanic service. Moreover, I am ashamed to admit that neither my mother nor I had ever learned how to change a tire, so we were forced to sit on the side of the road until a transport truck driver passing by was kind enough to stop and help us change the flat tire – in the dark, with below-freezing temperatures. It was really a generous labour on his part!

When we eventually made it up to Kapuskasing, I found out I was to be competing with another girl who had come in by *plane* for the interview. Fortunately, I ended up landing the job, and I was glad our 11 hours in the car was not in vain (although I can't say I felt good about having taken the job from the poor lady who flew in by plane!). Securing this job would lead to another long drive back up to the town a month later, only for the second trip, I was alone with Gordon Lightfoot blaring through the speakers of my old Ford Pinto. I cried the whole way there. I had never left Kingston before, and now it seemed I was venturing out, alone, to a place where I knew absolutely no one.

I believe a few of my old Red Baron teammates had bet money on how long I'd last up in the north before I came running back home to Mama Kingston. Well, I only lasted three years before their predictions were proven correct, but a lot can happen in three years. I admit I was a bit of a spoiled brat before I left, being the youngest of seven, a real "mommy's little girl." This trip, however, had a profound impact on the development of my character. All of the sudden, I'd cut all the ties in my social network, and was henceforth made to provide for myself. It was definitely a turning point between my childhood and my future as an adult.

Thankfully, my network would not remain empty long. Shortly after arriving in my new town, I heard tell of a women's hockey team that was run by the local surgeon, Dr. Ben Walker. Dr. Walker had two daughters who played on the team, which consisted mainly of high-school girls who spoke English, French, or a jargon somewhere in between. The team was about as ragged and shoddy as you can imagine – even worse than the Red Barons. Some of the equipment those girls had dug up was so ratty that it was practically beginning to disintegrate.

Likewise, the quality of their play was somewhat lacking in sparkle, although their character certainly was not! I thoroughly enjoyed our Sunday morning practices, which were like a breath of fresh air, as all the girls made up for their poor technique by playing with spirit and heart. Their mediocre skill level was hardly surprising, considering the girls only practiced once a week and were lucky to get a game in if they could. The only teams they had to face were local boys' teams, along with three distant women's teams: one from Smooth Rock Falls, 45 minutes away, another in Iroquois Falls, two hours away, and the third in Hearst, about an hour away, but that was only when Hearst had a team to play against, which wasn't guaranteed every year.

I had decidedly left my competitive player days behind when I moved up to Kapuskasing, but I couldn't resist the pull of the game forever. After a few months, I ended up taking over from the busy Dr. Walker as coach of the team. However, Dr. Walker was still well involved with our program, not only as a parent, but also as an informal trainer! He was especially helpful when we had to hand over his daughter Wendy after she broke her collarbone during a game in Iroquois Falls, our only major injury while I was coaching. I don't think we could have put Wendy in better care!

The girls were all hopeful that with my experience in hockey, particularly women's hockey, I might be able to help organize the team enough to bring it to the next level. I don't know if I ever succeeded in this endeavour, but I decided to bring the girls to their first ever tournament: our annual Red Baron tourney down in Kingston! The girls were elated. For some, this was the first time they had ever left Northern Ontario.

Girls' teams back then tended to be smaller, usually only about 10-12 girls and a goalie, so we were all able to pile into my car and a friend's minivan and drive down Highway 11 until we hit the "big city." I think the girls were pretty much last place in the tourney, but I was so proud of the effort they put in, and they were ecstatic to be playing against new teams at their level. On the last day, I took them all over to my old homestead after we checked out of the hotel, and my mother cooked us a big bacon and egg breakfast before the long ride back.

It was a hard life in Northern Ontario, and some of these girls really needed the break from town that stay-away tournaments like this offered, along with the distraction that a good game of hockey provided. I remember one girl by the name of Debbie who particularly benefited from this kind of support.

Debbie was so personable and absolutely loved hockey, but she didn't have the best home life to return to after practice. Her father and brother were notorious drunks, and Debbie would later follow in their footsteps. I felt for her, considering the home life I came from. I remember the role Annabelle and Cookie had played for me, and I tried to help her in a similar way. I believe Debbie was truly trying to make a better life for herself, but it didn't seem to ever work out. The poor kid never had any breaks, and I couldn't seem to find a way to help her like I wanted. She loved hockey and she loved our team, but obviously the game wasn't enough to intercede completely. I kept in touch with Debbie for many years after I moved away until she unfortunately passed on a few years ago.

It was in 1976, just a few weeks after I moved up north, that I got a call from my old friend Cookie asking if I would be interested in holding a volunteer position as the northern representative for the newly-formed Ontario Women's Hockey Association, the OWHA. At that time, on top of coaching the women's team, I was the director of the North Eastern Ontario Recreation Council, run by the Ministry of Culture and Recreation, so I was in a good position to understand the dynamics of women's hockey in the area. I readily agreed to take the position alongside Cookie on the OWHA executive board, where she was President for the first year and a bit. A few years later, I would be chosen as the VP for the association by President Frank Champion-Demers, after his election in 1978.

Established on September 6, 1975, the OWHA was the first ever government-funded and provincially-recognized organization for women's hockey in Ontario. It had formed in the wake of a letter received by Mr. Jim Coutts of the Ministry of Sport and Recreation, from one Ms. Susan Dalziel of Prince Edward Island. Ms. Dalziel had inquired about the status of women's hockey in Ontario, and as to whether there was a provincial organization which might be interested in interacting with her women's hockey association in P.E.I.

This was a turning point for the provincial government, which henceforth decided that, like they had done for ringette 10 years earlier, they should provide funding and support for the growing women's hockey program in Canada. This public sponsorship was an important development for women in hockey, because it gave girls in the sport a sort of validity or legitimacy which we had not enjoyed up until that point.

The provincial government set aside a grant of $3,000 to cover the start-up costs of the organization. By doing so, they put our program above all the other women's hockey organizations that were just beginning to settle into the province. They asked Cookie Cartwright if she would incorporate the association and begin with the task of getting the program up and running.

Cookie accepted the proposal and began by sending out flyers to the some 200-odd hockey teams she knew of, asking them to meet up at the Brampton Dominion Tournament hosted by women's hockey icon Fran Rider, to discuss the possibility of organizing a cohesive association. Cookie coordinated a working volunteer force comprised of an executive committee and district representatives, and together, we started to identify leagues and teams in Ontario and approach them about joining the OWHA. We were tight on cash but excited about the prospect of what was to come. I remember Waldo Henderson, our government consultant with the Ministry of Culture and Recreation, sternly reprimanded us one time us for being off budget by *one cent* in our first or second year. I don't think we could really call him much of a fan of women's hockey! But we didn't let little things like that bother us. We had important work to do.

A year or so later, Cookie, knowing she didn't have the time or the secretarial support required to run the program, stepped down and nominated Celia Southward as the new president. Celia was a valuable asset to the group as she was working at that time for Windsor Parks and Recreation, which meant she had access to the typewriters and photocopiers that were necessary to facilitate our ever-growing body of players. With this equipment, Celia was able to start the OWHA newsletter, which was distributed to all our sanctioned teams and anyone else who was interested in women's hockey.

The newsletter was a short document, only a few pages long, which featured information about upcoming OWHA-sanctioned tournaments, recent league and lead player stats, and opportunities for women and their supporters to be involved in government-funded coach, trainer, and referee certification programs. It also encouraged young girls and their parents to try to increase public awareness for the women's game by, for example, notifying local media of their playoff results, writing to Cooper about not discontinuing their line of girls' hockey equipment, or talking to their local OHA (Ontario Hockey Association – the boys' version of the OWHA), or CAHA (Canadian Amateur Hockey Association) representatives about girls' hockey.

The letter also pushed teams to fight for the rights to icetime at their local arenas by asking for a proportional icetime allotment in relation to the number of teams who shared the rink. There was a real shortage of rinks across the province in the 1970s and '80s, even for men. The provincial government created a lottery called *Wintario* during this time, to help fund the building of new recreation facilities and rinks, amongst other things. However, before there were enough rinks available for everyone, the girls often got the short end of the stick when it came to getting our fair share of hours on the ice.

In Kapuskasing, we were lucky enough to have a fantastic rink manager, Nick Ruckavina, who always made sure we got our icetime. However, this was almost unusual in the world of women's hockey in the 1970s, as boys generally were put ahead of girls in terms of scheduling priorities because their games were seen as simply being more important than girls'. Some people even had the nerve to argue that by playing hockey, we were taking away from the icetime that "rightfully" belonged to boys.

One newsletter in 1978 also contained our own version of the "Coach's Corner," where we specified activities that could help girls keep up their fitness up during the offseason. Among soccer, biking, and other summer sports recommended, the letter contained the following quote about strength training for girls:

> "Girls' shooting is usually poor because of a lack of such [upper body] strength – even push-ups can overcome this. Start with 2 or 3 a day and add one every other day – done 2 to 3 times a day, they'll be amazed how much improvement is shown by September – as well as firming up their busts!"

It still blows my mind that we had to advertise an exercise that would "firm up their busts" to get girls to try some off-season strength training. We had to make it into a new way to be "pretty" in order for the concept to be popular. Unlike today, very few people found girls to even more beautiful for their strength. Looking back, I don't know why we ever thought it was a good idea to have to made such a statement!

All flaws aside, these newsletters were a great advancement for women's hockey in Ontario, because they were the first form of organized communication between a large body of sanctioned teams and a central governing power in the girls' sport. They helped us reach our goal of creating a comprehensive provincial playdown for women in the province, and the two-way communication helped to categorize our teams by age and skill level. These categories were necessary in order to foster an infrastructure of more competitive games, which would in turn help to increase the overall skill level of women's hockey in Ontario.

Along with the creation of these newsletters, Celia Southward had a lasting impact on the OWHA thanks to her exceptional networking skills. Celia helped to expand the number of district representatives across the province to reach more girls in an increasingly extensive web of teams and leagues.

One of the individuals to help Celia in this endeavour was Mr. Carl Noble, then President of the North Metro Girls' Hockey Association, who became one of the earliest members of the OWHA. Carl was a firefighter by trade who had become involved in women's hockey when his four-year-old daughter saw a registration stand for a Newtonbrook girls' team at a shopping mall in 1967. He would support his daughter as a parent, and later as an administrator, before he was asked to join the OWHA as the district representative for the North Metro area, almost a decade after his debut as a volunteer in the sport.

Carl quickly moved up the ranks of the OWHA and took on the role of Registration Coordinator before becoming President in the early 1980s. As Registration Coordinator, Carl developed players' cards for all the women in the program. These cards were about the size of a credit card and made out of heavy paper. They featured the woman's name and a unique registration number for each player, which made it easier for the girl to sign up for future tournaments, and for us to keep track of all the players and teams. The only problem Carl had with the cards was when young women got married, changed their last name without notifying us, and then tried to register for a tournament with a new name the next year! We had a hard time figuring out who was who!

Carl continued to use this carding system – one of the only of its kind for any sport in Ontario at the time – until 1991, when he retired from women's hockey. At that point, Carl had to enlist the assistance of his more tech-savvy neighbour to help him for several hours a day to put the carding information into a digital format, because the number of registered girls had grown exponentially, from about 50 to 1,500 hundred teams, during the decade and a half that the OWHA had been in existence.

In 1977, after the OWHA had been around for about two years, the CAHA recognized that more and more girls were playing hockey in the country, and they decided that they should organize a meeting to identify and address the issues faced by the women's hockey programs in Canada. They called a three-day "study session" in late October, and we were all hopeful that the CAHA might decide to take us under their wing and finally support a national program for women alongside the men.

Sadly, nothing much resulted from the meeting, other than the general agreement that sanctioning women's hockey posed too many problems to solve at that point. They were still scratching their heads about what to do with all of us women playing a man's sport. All the same, we weren't dejected by the CAHA's neglect for our program. As women in hockey, we had grown up learning how to fend for ourselves, and we would eventually fight our way into the male federal governing body just a few years down the road.

After Celia Southward, a man by the name of Frank Champion-Demers was elected president in 1978, and chose me to be his Vice President for the new term. I was very happy to become more involved in the program, and I worked well with the President. Frank was originally from Ottawa, and had graduated from the Royal Military College in 1956. He had become involved in girls' hockey thanks to his daughter Cathy's interest in the sport. Since there was no girls' league in Nepean for Cathy to play in at the time, Frank organized a team for his daughter and some of her friends, who had only had the chance to play on local outdoor rinks in the 1960s.

Frank continued to volunteer his time to build the women's program in Ottawa, and his efforts earned him a spot on the OWHA Council as the Ottawa district rep before his promotion to President. He was a valuable asset to have on our team because he worked in communications for Corrections Canada at the time, and his office secretary was able to take over the newsletter and take messages when Frank was on the road, which happened quite a bit.

During my time as second to Frank Champion-Demers, we were mainly fighting the attitudes of parents who still thought that girls shouldn't play hockey. Along with Carl Noble, our bookkeeper and secretary Bev Mallory, district reps Dave Pollock from London, Don Hines from Chatham, Celia Southward from Windsor-Sarnia, Richard Gibbard from Kingston, Deb Adams from Cornwall, Wendy O'Connell from Huntsville, and Don Arnaud from Lakefield, we had built a solid foundation of sanctioned leagues from all across the province. Our program now including thousands of players from strong groups such as Carl Noble's North Metro Girls' Hockey Association, and Frank's Ottawa District Women's Hockey Association.

We had developed a provincial championship playdown tournament for teams of all different skill and age levels, representing some of the best female hockey in the province. We had organized all the girls under the same set of rules and standards across all our leagues, so everyone played the same game with the same equipment (for simplicity's sake, we had decided to follow the CAHA standard rules, checking included, with a few minor safety exceptions such as increased time for some penalties and a few more pieces of mandatory equipment). The task now was to make hockey uniformly socially acceptable, to which end we organized a campaign around the motto: "*Of course, girls play hockey, too.*" The final step was to expand our program so as to make it as comprehensive as possible.

We actually had a hard time convincing Fran Rider, the current President of the OWHA and her Brampton Canadettes Girls' Hockey Association to join in our program. Fran's Canadettes hosted the annual Easter "Dominion" Tournament I so loved, which some considered the closest thing to a Canadian Women's Nationals. However, it should be noted that this was an invitational tournament with no provincial playdowns or sanctioning from a recognized hockey body.

Although she had shown initial interest in the idea at the meeting organized by Cookie, Fran later refused to have her tournament sanctioned by the OWHA, as she didn't see any value in joining our association. Numerically, the Brampton Girls' Hockey Association was nearly as large as the entire OWHA, but it wasn't supported by the government, and didn't include teams from outside the Brampton area. We had to almost blackmail Fran into joining our group, because the provincial organization needed her support due to the sheer size of her association. It would have been a great loss to not have the Brampton girls compete with all the other teams in our program.

Carl Noble and I both remember that we had to tell our sanctioned players that if they participated in Fran's tournament, we wouldn't allow them to compete in our provincial playdowns. It was a bit of a cheap shot, I know, but we were left with very few other options to convince Brampton to join us. We forced our players through this ultimatum for many years and still Fran refused to yield, until finally, after we had organized a successful first women's National Championship in 1982, Brampton agreed to come on board. After that, Fran quickly rose through the ranks, and has since worked miracles for the women's hockey program on the international stage.

For the entirety of my involvement in the OWHA until 1979, I had remained working for the Board of Education up in Kapuskasing. Well, needless to say, the winters up there are rough and really take their anger out on the backs of the people, myself included. After three years, when I realized there were no better jobs to be had in the area, I was ready to come back to Kingston. My old Red Baron girlfriends had won their bet after all: I was headed home to Southern Ontario to look for new opportunities.

Although I was sad to leave my Kapuskasing girls' team behind, I was glad to be on familiar turf once more, although it wasn't the same now that many of my old friends had moved away. I didn't take long to settle into my old routines, and the next thing I knew, just a few months later, I had a new job. I started working full-time for the Hockey Ontario Development Committee as the first ever salaried female employee dedicated to women's hockey in Canada.

VII

Working for the
Hockey Ontario Development Committee

"Rhonda Leeman expects to wake up one day and find a boy who wants to join the Ontario Women's Hockey Association. Should that happen, she will know she is doing a good job." 43

-Robert McKenzie, Sports Journalist. 1981.

In the wake of an era of extreme aggression in professional hockey, as demonstrated by groups such as the notorious Philadelphia Broad Street Bullies, or by lesser-known individuals in amateur hockey leagues across the country, the Ministry of Community and Social Services of Ontario partnered with the Ministry of Sport and Recreation to commission a research project on the status of violence in hockey, in accord with Section 7 of the Athletics Control Act. This resulted in the publication of the *Investigation and Inquiry into*

---

43 McKenzie, Robert. "Hockey for Girls Gains Momentum." *The Globe and Mail* [Toronto], 22 Sept. 1981.

Violence in Amateur Hockey, a report completed in 1974 by the Honourable William R. McMurtry.[44]

The report scrutinizes an incident of exceptional violence in a Bramalea boys' minor hockey program which acutely prompted the proposal for inquiry, as well as the causal relationships that underlay the general brutality of the sport in the 1970s. The report found that there was a lack of training for coaches and education for parents about the real values of the game. This lacuna had resulted in a plethora of people who had become so focused on winning and "going pro" that they were pushing their kids to become elite players at all costs, which often led to extremely aggressive situations.

McMurtry put forth a handful of recommendations that could help to reduce this agitation in minor hockey leagues. These suggestions included defining the purposes of the sport, reworking the rulebook to crack down on fighting, implementing mandatory coaching, refereeing, and trainer certification programs, educating parents and fans about the innate values of the sport at a non-competitive level, helping the media to understand the role they play in the glorification of the violence in professional hockey, and implementing a council which could help to materialize the preceding articles and manage the sport in the future.

These recommendations led to the development of the Ontario Hockey Council in 1979, which became the Hockey Ontario

44 The inquiry is a 40-page document available online. See http://www.ontla.on.ca/library/repository/mon/25005/32920.pdf if you'd like to browse through the report yourself.

Development Committee (HODC) in the 1980s, and is now known as the Hockey Development Centre for Ontario. This program was initially given $2 million in funding by the provincial government, allowing the council to hire a full-time representative for each official hockey organization in Ontario to start implementing the changes McMurtry put forth.

Since the report had specified that these adjustments were to benefit *all* hockey players, and since the OWHA had recently been validated as a legitimate organization for women hockey players in the province, we pushed for a development coordinator for the female program to be hired alongside those of the men's program. But even though there were six recognized hockey associations in the province at the time, only four development coordinators were hired in total: one each for the OWHA, the North Ontario Hockey Association (NOHA), the Thunder Bay Hockey Association (TBHA), and the Ottawa District Hockey Association (ODHA), because the Metro Toronto Hockey League (MTHL) did not recognize the Development Committee and the Ontario Minor Hockey Association (OMHA) recognized the Committee but refused to hire a Coordinator.

Naturally, I jumped at the chance to have an official job in the women's hockey sector and applied for the female Coordinator position along with 30 or so other individuals. Initially, I was chosen as the runner-up for the post, just behind a man by the name of Bob Headley. Bob was an instructor at Durham College who was high up in the hockey world at that time, and I would bet that he was offered the job in accordance with the politics of the day. But Bob had a family to feed, and when he found out that the job only paid $25,000 per year and that the contract only lasted three years, he declined the offer and I was given the position. As VP for the OWHA, with a BA and 12 years of experience in women's hockey by that point, I figured I was more qualified for the job than Bob anyways, and I accepted the proposition.

I started working in 1980 and quickly learned that there were actually two parts to the job. Don Robb, executive director of the HODC, seemed to think I should follow in the footsteps of the other development coordinators he had hired for the program, whereas my old boss Frank Champion-Demers seemed to think that the paid position allowed me to work full-time for the OWHA, even though I had had to resign from my position as VP to accept the title of Development Coordinator. Frank treated my position more like an executive director, which meant that I had more responsibility than what was actually spelled out in my job description. Moreover, it meant that I did administrative work for the OWHA – something that the HODC didn't really appreciate.

While the HODC wanted me to push out certification programs for trainers, coaches, and referees, the OWHA expected me to push their program to a higher level of respectability by identifying as many girls' teams as possible and helping them to them affiliate with our organization. It was a tricky situation; it seemed to me that Frank would often be mad at me for one thing, and Don would be mad at me for something else, because I found it extremely difficult to fulfill both of their conflicting expectations!

97

I ended up doing both jobs as best I could and tried to shoulder the flak from my supervisors. In November and December of 1980, I once again took my Ford Pinto on two lonely month-long road trips across Northern Ontario, driving for what seemed like an eternity to talk to rink managers and Parks and Rec staff in every town, trying to find out if they were aware of any girls' teams in their areas. Some could put me in contact with well-organized teams or even entire leagues, which I could then approach about joining our association, but sometimes all the rink managers could do was to point me towards a handful of women who took to the ice to play shinny once in a while. These girls often had no idea they were not alone and that there was another handful of unorganized girls playing the same game only two or three towns over.

The trip led me to places like Dryden, Kenora, Fort Frances, Thunder Bay, Sault Ste Marie, and even a few nearby First Nations. I often had success in affiliating new teams with the OWHA, but it was sometimes hard to get the more distant teams to affiliate with our organization because the travel costs to compete in our leagues and tournaments were too substantial to make it worth their while. Many asked me for funding to help with equipment and other expenses, but I had nothing to offer. The most I could do was invite them to refereeing or coaching clinics usually held a few hours away, put them in contact with other girls' teams that they could play in towns nearby, and make note of their numbers for our records.

It was in keeping track of these numbers that I began to realize just how many girls were already involved in the sport across the province. I was astounded by the frequency of towns with women players. Before I'd left, the OWHA had only registered 101 teams. But by the time I came back, we had a total of 203 teams associated with our organization, and around 12,000 female hockey players in all. It was over the course of this trip, taking in the abundance of smiling female faces, that I became incredibly infatuated with the idea of providing a comprehensive program to support these women in their goals, a structure which could further their involvement in the sport.

I tried to speak to the local media in each town – newspaper, radio, television, and anyone else who would listen to me[45] – to help raise awareness about the lack of support for their local girls' teams and see if I could find any sponsors. This advocacy, however, caused some problems because a lot of men's hockey programs were reluctant to support us, seeing as it meant having to share icetime, grants, and sponsorships. The way they saw it, girls already had ringette and figure skating, both of which took away from their practice time and resources, and which were "more feminine anyways."

The OWHA was different from the other hockey organizations in Ontario in the sense that it had jurisdiction over all the province, whereas the different men's organizations each had a certain territory to govern. This meant that wherever we went, the

---

[45] See https://www.cbc.ca/player/play/1586099799 for an interview I did about women's hockey on CBC's *Take Thirty*, 17 Feb. 1983.

OWHA encroached on the territory of the male association in the region, and this caused quite a few issues for us.

I recall one weekend in Cornwall where we had brought in our staff to run a development clinic for coaches, trainers, and referees in the women's program in the area. Cornwall was ODHA territory at that time, and the ODHA was certainly upset that we had brought in instructors loyal to the OWHA to run the weekend, because they considered this to be their territory and, thus, they thought we had no right to use *our* people on *their* turf, even though we were there to work with people in a different program! This is yet another prime example of certain men not being able to understand that a women's organization could be just as competent and powerful as their own. Thankfully, there wasn't much they could do about the situation, and we used our staff despite their territorial quibbling.

Along with the difficulties faced in the implementation of these development programs, we had some trouble with the creation of the course materials themselves, particularly in the Trainer development program, now known as the Hockey Trainer Certification Program, or HTCP. When we were designing a training manual for the women's program, many individuals argued that the manual needed coverage of injuries "specific" to the female body. Most of these "specific injuries," however, were pure nonsense. They wanted us to make a big deal about how to properly attend to an athlete suffering from "debilitating" period cramps, and again, the question was brought up about what to do if a female player developed breast cancer from being hit in the chest with a puck.

As an interlude, an equally ridiculous situation that stands out clearly in my memory occurred during the summer of 1981, when I was the only woman working at the HODC Huron Hockey School up in Grand Bend, Ontario. Skill-wise, I held my own pretty well with the rest of the male coaches – I implemented some technical skill workshops that went over successfully with the staff and students.

However, when we had finished working one night, the other coaches and I left our hotel to walk to a restaurant for dinner. The "bro culture" still being highly present in hockey at the time, I was horrified but hardly surprised when one of my male colleagues, an NHL coach, thought it funny to get ahead of me, drop his pants, and *moon* me in front of the rest of his hockey buddies as we were crossing the parking lot to the restaurant.

Of course, all my male colleagues found the joke highly entertaining, although I can't say I shared in their opinion. It was highly unprofessional and contributed to the sense of exclusion and mockery I was already experiencing as the only woman at the camp. I hope that today, if that same incident were to occur, one of my male colleagues would stand up and support me while I gave that hoser a piece of my mind.

Thankfully, there were a few individuals in the HODC who were very supportive of our work, and who looked past gender stereotypes and foolish notions about breast cancer to provide invaluable contributions to the establishment of our program, and the HTCP.

One individual that deserves special recognition in the HTCP area was Bob Firth, the man who spearheaded the program's whole production. Bob was an incredible trainer and must have looked after thousands of players over the course of his career. Regrettably, Bob passed away early in life from a sickness that no one could identify at the time. In hindsight, many speculate that the illness was an autoimmune disease transmitted by one of the many players Bob had stitched up without the gloves which are now a mandatory part of all emergency medical interventions. Bob's invaluable contribution to the advancement of the trainer program will never be forgotten, and he will live on in the hearts of all the individuals that his work has since helped save. Unfortunately, Bob never had the joy of seeing the certification program he developed reach the national level, as he died only three years after the program was launched provincially.

I remember attending a Toronto Blue Jays' game with Bob and some of the other Development Coordinators and administrators from the CAHA. Bob still looked fairly healthy at that point, but he was always complaining of something – everything seemed to nag at him. It was my very first time seeing the Blue Jays play, and I remember the snowy April day very clearly. That was one of the perks I received now that I was part of the group of paid hockey administrators. We were seated in the box of the Labatt Brewing Co. – fantastic seats – thanks to the sponsorship deal the company had just signed with Canada's hockey and baseball big wigs.

Yet in spite of this high-profile treatment, there were still hockey people in this era who had no idea that an association for women even existed. I remember calling a certain minor hockey representative from Peterborough in the early '80s to see if they had any information about the status of women's hockey in the district, and was humbled to hear him demand *"The who?!"* after I'd introduced myself as a representative of the OWHA. And there I was, thinking we had made some headway in the sport, only to realize in that moment that we would be fighting this uphill battle for many years to come.

Nonetheless, I was proud of the progress we had made. The CAHA estimated at this point that there were about 25,000 girls playing organized hockey in Canada, and I knew that number was growing. What we needed now was to provide a competitive structure for these women and girls, something that could bring our status up to equality with that of the men. We needed to bring women's hockey to the next level.

VIII

Organizing a National Women's Tournament

I recall a sunny September day in 1979 after an OWHA meeting in Toronto when I had a discussion over lunch with President Frank Champion-Demers about the possibility of organizing a legitimate national hockey tournament for women in Canada. We realized it was our mutual dream to be able to provide young girls in the sport with a competitive infrastructure that mirrored that of the men.

We talked about the possibility of taking the creation of this infrastructure into our own hands – of organizing a national-level event of some kind – although at the time this idea was little more than a pipedream to us. However, in the 1980-81 season, as I was nearing the completion of my team recruitment tours up North for the HODC, Frank and I started talking about the next big project we wanted to undertake in women's hockey, and the dream resurfaced.

We realized that the advantages such a project offered were extraordinary and began seriously considering the possibility of organizing a women's nationals in late 1981. A national championship would give girls in hockey a real goal to reach for in the sport – it would become the incentive they needed to keep pushing their limits and expanding their horizons, and it would create positive role models for younger players to look up to in the sport. It could also act as a sort of vault towards a potential international professional league for women, one step closer to reaching a status of equality with men.

We reckoned that a national championship would also benefit girls' hockey by attracting the attention of media from across the country. Good coverage of the tournament could help to convince our critics that women's hockey was a sport to be taken just as seriously as that of our male counterparts. Using media to decrease the social stigma around women playing hockey would allow more girls the chance to participate in the sport.

As the 1981 holiday season approached, Frank decided that the first step to putting our project into action was to recruit a few strong advocates who would be able to vouch for our cause and provide a support network to get us going.

The first person we decided to contact was Mrs. Maureen McTeer, wife of future Prime Minister Joe Clarke, the leader of the Federal opposition at the time. Maureen had played hockey as a young girl in the Ottawa Valley and had dreamed of playing in the NHL, until she was reminded by her father that she was female and girls were not welcome in the league. Despite, or perhaps because of this childhood setback, Maureen proved more than willing to help our cause when I met with her in late December. She was delighted at the chance to bring her old dream closer to reality for women in the future.

With people like Maureen behind us, Frank announced to the rest of the OWHA in late December 1981 that we were going to develop the first ever Women's National Hockey Tournament, which would be held in April of 1982. I was named chairperson for the event in mid-January 1982, after which we really started really putting in the hours to get this dream out of the dirt and growing.

I had to request permission from my HODC supervisor Don Robb to devote my time to organizing this important milestone for women, and he accepted, giving the event at least one full-time employee. But we were still very short on cash, and although Don agreed to pay my hours working on the project, he made it very clear that the rest of the tournament was not going to be run at the expense of the HODC.

Nor was the tournament going to be funded by the OWHA. Our organization had little more than a few grand in its coffers at the time, and we knew we were going to be needing some serious financial assistance to defray expenses like insurance coverage, advertising efforts, renting arenas and banquet halls, paying referees and rink staff, and helping with the travel and accommodations of the players. This last point was especially important, because we didn't want the financial burden to keep anyone from making it to the tournament.

We talked to Maureen about the issue of expenses, and she helped us by writing a letter requesting financial assistance on our behalf to Abby "Ab" Hoffman – the little girl who had been kicked off of the boys' team in 1956 and had subsequently gone on to compete at four Olympics and become the first female Director of Sport Canada. Thankfully, Abby agreed to come on board, and helped us access funding in the form of a grant from Sport Canada, and get official sanctioning from the CAHA (see appendix D).

The CAHA's official recognition and the Sport Canada grant were two essential and intertwined elements of our project. Once Abby was on board, she asked the CAHA to sanction and support our event. The CAHA, however, thought that their purse should only be opened for those who were already enrolled in their association (that is, the boys), and so didn't offer us any funding personally, and were very reluctant to sanction our event.

The CAHA's aversion to supporting us was not, apparently, because they were opposed to girls in hockey, but rather because there "weren't enough" funds and icetime for both men and women to play. On January 13, 1982, we received a letter from Ron Robinson, senior CAHA marketing and communications assistant, who specified that the organization wanted "the women's program be added to the CAHA operational budget but not at the expense of ongoing [boys'] programs." Essentially, they were afraid that a women's hockey program would take away from the men – and because men were seen as having more right to icetime, many saw this as a reasonable excuse to deny girls a chance to play. Thankfully, after an extensive letter campaign by myself and Frank Champion-Demers, and a lot of pushing from Abby Hoffman at Sport Canada, the CAHA agreed to sanction us. However, this concession was only given on the following conditions:

1. We had to organize a structured provincial playdown for each province to make the tournament legitimate;

2. We had to identify a representative for the female hockey program in each province in order to create a country-wide communication network to help govern women's hockey;

3. The CAHA had to receive a $5,000 grant from Sport Canada which they could then give to us to put towards the tournament.

Meanwhile, Abby had written to us that the tournament *had* to occur with CAHA sanctioning in order to receive the grant money requested from her, and so we found ourselves stuck in a bit of a bureaucratic logjam that took a lot of hassle to work through.

In the end, we secured the grant-sanctioning combo after a few headache-filled weeks of meetings and letter exchanges extremely late in the organizational process – only about a month and a half before the event was scheduled to take place. Thank goodness we had decided to proceed with or without the CAHA's sanctioning, and had made progress with other preparations.

We knew this $5,000 from Sport Canada was not going to be near enough money to cover the whole cost of a national-level tournament, so we started looking for other possible sponsorship opportunities. We concluded that we should try to find a corporate sponsor, although we didn't know exactly how to go about doing that.

It may sound crazy in this day and age, but I ended up knocking on the doors of a half-dozen big brand-name corporations to ask if their companies would be willing to sponsor our Championship. I literally walked into these impressive corporate boardrooms holding nothing more than an audacious vision and a few press clippings about the growth in popularity of women's hockey in the nation.

Not surprisingly, I was very nervous about this risky marketing move because we had extremely little to offer potential sponsors in exchange for their financial support – no benefits, no prime ad exposure, not even a guaranteed audience! I remember we attempted to list the few perks that came with funding our program on a bulletin we sent out to potential sponsors, but the best I could come up with was: "Girls' hockey is a very controversial issue." Effectively, all I had to offer was the publicity these companies might get from supporting the "controversy" of women playing a "man's sport."

Not a single corporation agreed to even entertain a discussion about possible sponsorship opportunities until I walked into the Shoppers Drug Mart head office. Shoppers agreed to sign on to a major three-tier, three-year sponsorship deal for the first Women's Nationals, which henceforth became known as the "Shoppers Drug Mart Women's Nationals." They were truly a blessing for our tournament. It is very doubtful that we would have been able to make the event work at all without their help.

The sponsorship we acquired was quite impressive, far beyond what we had originally imagined possible. Shoppers agreed to help us at the local, provincial, and national levels: they provided money to support our tournament, as well as money to help each of the provincial playdowns, and, most importantly, they promised to sponsor a local girls' hockey team for the next three years in every town where they had a store location. In return, we gave them media exposure at our tournament, designed a special logo for the event with their brand on it, and printed the logo on jerseys and posters to advertise for the weekend (see appendix C).[46]

David Shelton, the CMO of Shoppers at the time, became our point of contact in the company. David was extremely helpful to us – he managed to get us television coverage on the *Wide World of Sports*, and two of the coaches from the tournament featured on *Canada AM.*

Television coverage of this sort had been part of the contract I'd signed with Shoppers, even though at the time I had absolutely no idea how I was going to go about obtaining such a thing. Never before had women's hockey been televised! But I'd closed my eyes and signed away, deciding we would make it happen somehow. My intuition proved correct – David Shelton helped us find the airtime we needed to fulfill our contract, and get women's hockey across to a national public audience.

---

[46] I've never been much of an artist so I was very thankful that Shoppers had specialists available to help us design the logo!

It was such a relief to have Shoppers Drug Mart agree to a sponsorship, although the fact that we secured the deal only five weeks before we dropped the puck meant I didn't get much sleep until after the tournament!

Once Shoppers was on board, they helped us obtain grants from Planter's Peanuts, Scott Paper, and Lifebrand, which came on as secondary sponsors for the tourney. With this decent financial foundation lined up, I was able to confidently sign contracts with arenas, banquet halls, insurance companies, etc., and start working in overdrive to fit all the other pieces in place.

The grant money we obtained from Sport Canada was used to help defray travel and meal expenses for players outside a radius of 160 km round trip from the event. It also went towards organizing the provincial playdowns that had to be held prior to the Nationals to ensure we received the very best teams from each province.

These playdowns were another big problem we had to think through, a problem which wasn't made easier by the tight timeline of the event. We had to make sure that every province was able to execute a legitimate qualifying tournament within a month after deciding we were going to have the championship, because we needed the names of the teams and players in order to arrange their airfare. Despite this, some provinces only confirmed their attendance as late as March 3. I suppose that isn't surprising considering we were asking these provinces to come up with a provincial championship in the middle of playoff season, and during a time when ice for girls was nearly impossible to come by!

Maureen had been kind enough to write on our behalf to the Minister of Sport and Recreation in every province before we'd even obtained the deal with Shoppers Drug Mart. She asked if the ministries would be willing to provide any funding for their provincial playdowns or for the women's team from their province. Sadly, the response rate was less than satisfactory – Maureen reported on the responses she received in a letter to OWHA president Frank Champion-Demers, on February 24, 1982:

> "As you can see by their letters, neither Manitoba nor Saskatchewan will provide any money, which is most unfortunate. Their argument seems to be that the federal government should assume this funding for this kind of program; and that what monies they do have are better spent in other community related fields. I note with great irony the Manitoba suggestion that Ringette is better organized than women's hockey – as if the two should be mutually exclusive!"

Thankfully, a few provinces proved more receptive, and offered funding to help support their players, though often we had to meet a set of conditions which involved a good deal of bureaucratic gymnastics.

These playdowns were made all the more difficult to arrange due to the fact that many of their female athletes would have struggled to find resources like proper equipment in their hometowns, which also hindered the facilitation of many provincial tournaments.

112

The great geographic distances separating the provinces and our OWHA headquarters in Ontario was another challenge, because it meant communication travelled slowly, and organization took even longer to achieve. In those times, we had no emails, no fax, and no internet – everything was done manually with phone calls, telegrams and snail mail, which certainly didn't help to speed up the process. We had to travel everywhere to meet with people in person and our slide-shows were done on hand-drawn spreadsheets, with overhead projectors and Bristol board posters.

Thus, it was all the more exceptional to see the strings of a binding unity begin to form between the women in these provinces as, for the first time ever, women's hockey began to take the shape of a multi-fold tapestry of provincial and federal organizations.

Whereas once, many teams like Fran Rider's Brampton Canadettes hadn't joined the OWHA because they felt there was no benefit to being part of a program so far away or only slightly larger than their own, now the prospect of competing for a national title was just the incentive they needed to affiliate with the OWHA. This, in turn, advanced women's hockey in the long run because it created the infrastructure necessary to decide on consistent rules and competition levels, forming one unified system in both the province and the country – which, at the provincial level, is a feat that the boys' program has yet to achieve!

Due to our major lack of time and money, we decided to host the first Women's Nationals at the Brantford Arena because it was close to the airport. It was also already the home of a strong female hockey association, which could provide a solid base of volunteers to help pull off the championship.

We booked the players in 60 rooms in the Jolly Baron Inn – four girls per room – which was a convenient location because it was pretty close to the rink. We paid City Cab of Brantford $1.00 per drive to help run players back and forth to the arena, and we hired two pickup trucks to help cart all the players' equipment from the airport to Brantford and back, while the girls made the trip in four school buses from Parkinson Bus Lines. We had the St. John's ambulance and the Brantford General Hospital on standby during games, with Blue Cross for visitor coverage protection. Initially, we'd planned on using hockey trainers from a sports program at Sheridan College, but we couldn't secure a deal with them that would work with our limited budget.

We tried to make this event as professional as we could with the money and time we had, but more importantly, we wanted to give the athletes more than just a chance to play hockey at our tournament. Along with the games, we decided to run two clinics for girls who were interested, to finally give these women some decent coaching and practice time, seeing as resources were so hard to come by for most.

Al Taylor, a man who was then my boyfriend and later became my husband, was a certified coaching instructor and offered to roll up his sleeves and run an Early Bird Power Skating clinic for the first 30 women to register.[47]

We also had ex-NHL goalie Dave Dryden run a clinic for all the goaltenders and their coaches so they could learn valuable goalkeeper skills, which could then be passed on to more players in their home provinces. All involved in these two workshops had the opportunity to participate in a half hour of classroom time, plus an ice session with Dave and Al, and I would be willing to wager that this was the first time a lot of those goalies and players had ever had real skill-specific coaching instruction.

We offered both of these clinics free of charge in an attempt to help develop the skills that these women needed to form the foundation of a program that we hoped would someday be equal to that of the men.

Many of the players were ecstatic to have so many resources at their disposal for the first time in their hockey careers. Nonetheless, there were still many resources that we could not supply. The girls had to feed themselves, and a lot of them had to pay their travel fare. We could only afford to pay for about 50-60% of the players' airfare, thanks to the grant from Sport Canada and a secondary sponsorship from Air Canada that Abby Hoffman had managed to snag for us.

It's incredible to think that so many of these players chose to dip into their own pockets just to be a part of our event. But I find it

---

[47] Al has written a book entitled *So You Think You Can Skate*, which is available for all interested skating enthusiasts on Amazon.

even more incredible to think that the event was on a *national* scale, and these women still had to fundraise just to make it to the arena. I sincerely hope that our inability to provide adequate coverage for these girls didn't keep anyone from making it to the rink. We have to remember that every lost star is a lost step forward in the development of the sport, and the lack of funding for women even today continues to markedly hinder the advancement of our female athlete programs.

It took a lot of late nights from our team to put together the first National Women's Tournament – it was a big job to put together an event like that from scratch! Thankfully, we had a lot of volunteer help to alleviate the workload.

Carl Noble was highly instrumental in helping the event to take shape. Carl made sure that players abided by the CAHA stipulations and oversaw the Ontarian provincial qualifier playdowns.

Abby Hoffman sent us another guardian angel by the name of Cathy Lane MacDonald. Cathy was extremely useful in helping to fill out government forms and explaining to us the relationship between Sport Canada and the CAHA, which would have been something of a bureaucratic maze otherwise.

Another dedicated volunteer was Mr. Jerry Dalloway, owner of the Real McCoy Sports Store, who kindly agreed to supply equipment and skate sharpening services for the tournament at a 10% discount.

Jim Carmichael, the Administrative Chair of the tournament and President of the Brantford Girls' Hockey Association, was a

116

senior member of Harding Carpets, which was great because it meant we were henceforth able to hold all our board meetings in their office space. Jim and his righthand-man Bill Bishop, who was the Tournament Controller, were both excellent individuals who worked very hard to support the tournament in any way they could.

Bill especially was a good "money man." He knew our budget by heart. We owe much gratitude to Jim and Bill for all their hard work and dedication, as well as to Operating Chairperson John Stewart, the Logistics Chairperson Sharon Nicks, and the Tournament Co-Ordinator Don Arnaud, who was also a member of the OWHA executive board. Don was particularly invaluable in taking care of referees, time keepers, and other rink scheduling details to help make sure the operations at ice level occurred flawlessly.

Another member of our team was the arena manager in Brantford, Thelma Learn.48 Thelma was one of the few female arena managers in the province at the time, and had quite a few years' experience on the job. She embraced the women's championship wholeheartedly, but she had to make sure that our schedule wouldn't interfere with that of the OHL team in Brantford at the time, the Junior A Brantford Alexanders.

In terms of rink time, the Alexanders had priority over our tournament, even though we were organizing a national event and the Alexanders were not even in the playoff season. This disparity existed because the Alexanders were the number one source of revenue for

48 Not to be confused with Thelma, my car during the Red Barons era!

the arena. It is perhaps telling of the social system of the time that even a women's Nationals couldn't draw as many spectators as a regular boys' Junior A game. This unfortunate circumstance meant that Thelma had to find a weekend where the Alexanders wouldn't be playing at home, so that even if they made the playoffs, they would at least be away on the road, so we could use the arena.

Thelma also helped out a great deal with some of the more technical jobs that had to be completed to prepare the rink. Drawing the Shoppers' Championship logo at centre ice, for example, was something that I had no idea how to go about doing. Thelma also gave us a checklist of other tasks to accomplish around the rink, and it was always very clear that she would do anything she could do to help or, as she wrote to us at the end of the list mentioned above, "rest assured we will do our utmost to assist in assuring [the tournament's] success."

I would like to specifically recognize a volunteer by the name of Harry, whose last name I don't know but who was in charge of procuring the trophies we needed for the event. Harry's enthusiasm was extremely contagious – he was such a pleasure to work with. He took care of getting the tournament trophies – the "Abby Hoffman" cup for first place and the "Maureen McTeer" cup for second – and he was extremely helpful with a lot of other tasks. Harry's positive attitude is all the more inspiring considering he was most likely sick while he was working at the championship, although we didn't know it at the time. He died a year or so after the event, but his unflinching positivity has left an impression on me and others which shall not be forgotten.

The process of organizing such a major event could never have occurred without the hours put in by all these wonderful volunteers. They are the true foundation of the women's hockey program in Canada today.

However, being the only paid staff member, I have to admit it was rather troubling to think that any errors committed during the championship's organization would have come to rest on my neck. There were times where my 27-year-old-self naively signed my name to financial contracts that I had absolutely no means to pay should anything go south – many of the tournament's heftier expenses (booking arenas, banquet halls, and even the $1 million insurance waivers), carried my signature and my personal credit card number. Had the tournament failed, I would have been financially and socially responsible, and most likely used as the scapegoat for both the OWHA and the HODC. Thankfully, the volunteers at the Brantford Girls' Hockey Association and the OWHA did a fantastic job, and everything turned out exceptionally well, despite the bumps and bruises we had to overcome in the process.

Mind you, that didn't keep the squabbles between the OWHA and the HODC from giving me headaches for a few weeks. The HODC had not been very supportive of my efforts at running this event – the tournament was not what I had been hired to do, and the HODC management sure let me know it. On the other side, the OWHA was absolutely revelling at the sponsorship money coming in for the event, and my colleagues there started recommending all kinds of "fun" extra perks that we could do with the money. They just didn't seem to understand that I was barely coming in on budget as it was, and that we couldn't afford to add in all the frivolities suggested! And this is just a taste of the conflict I had to sort through on a daily basis.

Trying to find an adequate number of female referees to cover our games was definitely one of these bumps – another adventure wrought with stereotypes and sexism. Along with promoting women *playing* hockey, we had decided to have only female referees from each province *officiate* the games, to promote girls in other aspects of the sport as well. We had female referees come in for the games from all across the country, and we paid them using the grant from Sport Canada.

I found it surprising and disheartening to learn how few qualified female referees were actually out there. Many provinces reported that they did "not at present have any female officials in the province," and British Columbia only had one girl with the necessary level 2 certification, but she was only 17 so she would have needed time off school to attend. After much communication with hockey representatives from other provinces, we finally found and commissioned referees Barb Jeffrey, Debbie Smiley, Helen Murphy, and Monica Pollock as officials for our games. After that, Don Arnaud was tasked with the job of evaluating each referee that was able to attend, so that he could identify who was the best candidate for the championship game.

The decisions that had to be made regarding the playing equipment and playing rules for the tournament were other dilemmas we had to solve. The rules about body contact, especially, were tricky to pin down. Many female hockey leagues had decided to remove body contact from their games, be it due to the "traditional" idea that women were more likely to be injured than men, or simply as a safety precaution regardless of gender concerns. Moreover, this removal was done to varying degrees: some had removed only checking, some had removed all body contact, and some had even gone so far as to outlaw slapshots. But since our event had been officially sanctioned by the CAHA, we were bound to play under their rules for the tournament, meaning checking, slapshots, and body contact were all fair game.

Overall, in terms of the budget for the Women's Nationals, we made out pretty well considering the tight financial situation we'd faced at the beginning. Thanks to our sponsors and some minor income from ticket and merchandise sales, the total revenue we acquired amounted to approximately $61,500.[49] We managed to come in under budget at only $56,400 in expenses, and the $5,000 we made in profit during the tournament was given to the Brantford Girls' Hockey Association to put towards their programming.

This meager profit that we'd made mostly materialized at the rink level over the course of the weekend. We sold a few items at the tuck shop – drinks, snacks, Planter's Peanuts, crested pucks, crested

[49] Accounting for inflation, that amounts to over $130,000 today, which is not a very large amount of money to spend on a national-level event, considering some parents nowadays spend as much as $15,000 per year on one child alone in AAA hockey.

pennants and buttons inscribed with "I deserve this medal because I'm a hockey mom/dad." We even had a raffle draw for a new barbeque! But since we didn't have a lot of cash to put into buying memorabilia, our stock unfortunately sold out within the first few hours.

Similarly, ticket sales, at $2 per game for adults and $1 for students, provided another source of income, although it was equally trivial since our audience hardly filled the stands. In fact, the support we received from the public was so low that for the film coverage of the event, the cameraman asked the crowd to all sit on the same side of the stands, so he could film from the other and give the illusion that there were more people attending the games.

We knew that marketing an event like this would be the most challenging part of the whole project – we were well aware of the social stigma we were up against. We still had a hard time getting people to *accept* women playing hockey, never mind tuning in on TV or spending some money just to watch them play! But Frank and I felt that if we could get footage of what it actually looked like when women played the sport, we would be able to surprise a lot of individuals who had never seen a girl play. We hoped we could start a high-level education program for the general public, and show our country what quality hockey players they had in *all* their citizens.

Sweet Victory at the
World's First National Championship

It was specifically this kind of media coverage for the event that helped to make the tournament such a powerful push forward for women in sport, because it helped to change the stereotypes associated with women's hockey.

Knowing how important the media would be to the success of our tournament, I was really glad when Shoppers hired a public relations company – the Hilda Wilson Group – to help us to promote our story in newspapers, on the radio, on television, and at two press conferences we held before the tournament.

Since there was no big modern-style social media campaign to announce that the event was going to occur, and certainly no emails, websites or online reveals, these two press conferences were the only way to get the public's attention to focus on our tournament. It being a national event, we had a press conference for media from across the country at the Hot Stove Lounge in the old Maple Leaf Gardens in Toronto, followed by one for local media at the Iron Horse Restaurant in Brantford.

King Clancy, the famous NHL player and Vice President of the Toronto Maple Leafs, actually attended our press conference at the Hot Stove Lounge and helped promote the event. As a hockey legend from the "old days" when the NHL was still in its infancy, King Clancy was a smashing hit – and the best part was that we hadn't even invited him! Clancy happened to be walking past our room in the arena when we were having the conference and stopped in to check out the festivities!

When he learned what we were celebrating, Clancy came in and started speaking about his memories of women's hockey before the war, about the quality of their high-level play, and his delight at the resurgence in popularity of the sport during the last few years. He really was a wonderful gentleman – and after that day he became one of the strongest patrons of women's hockey in the country! He truly wanted to help our cause in any way he could.

In the end, it was the media coverage at the event that really added to the professionalism and synergy that helped me realize that our dream was coming true. We had *The Globe and Mail*, the *Toronto Star, Hockey News*, and other news corporations all attending the conference, which really helped make the tournament known to the public. I should mention that it was also the first time that the CAHA showed up to support any of our events.

Then, just a few days before the tournament, we held the second press conference at the Iron Horse Restaurant. This time, the (now infamous) hockey agent Alan Eagleson came to support us.[50] Maureen McTeer was able to call on Eagleson and ask him the favour of coming to the event, because he was a staunch conservative like her husband. Many of the local media from Kitchener, Simcoe, Hamilton, and Brantford also showed up, and a total of 33 news services from across the country either attended the conference in person or asked to have the information mailed to them so they could share our story in their local papers.

We had also arranged through the Hilda Wilson Group to have game results wired via telegraph to be aired on radio and television with the *Canadian Press, United Press of Canada, Broadcast News,* and *Standard Broadcast News* stations. *Standard Broadcast News* was connected with CFRB, as well as 57 other radio stations all across Canada, meaning people from sea to sea could keep up with the final scores at the end of every day.

As for the *Canadian Press* and the *United Press of Canada,* updates were supposed to be given to the sports desks after the first half and at the end of the match for games played on April 1-3, and more often for games played on the final day of the tournament, all describing not only the scores, but also some of the play and details concerning goals.

This kind of in-depth coverage was ground-breaking for women's hockey, since any coverage we had received in the past was usually more interested in how old the women were, whether they

---

[50] Note that this was *before* Eagleson had gotten himself in trouble with the law. At this time, his image had only a positive connotation in the hockey community.

were attractive, and then followed the humble opinion of the journalist about whether or not women should be allowed to play this "man's game."

However, despite achieving this kind of legitimate sports coverage for our tourney, the number of media outlets we had to call before any would commit to covering our event was atrocious, and it once again reminded us of the discrimination in media coverage for women's sports (which is rampant even today). Looking back on my notes, it is disheartening to see how many blatant "NO's" I had to inscribe beside the reporters we'd called. I counted 12 'NO's, and four 'Don't Know/Maybe's, on a page of only 26 total contacts. That's a positive response rate of only 38%.

Thankfully, the inequality was not nearly as bad at the ground level. At the rink, we were surrounded by people who were passionate about women's hockey. Positive energy was absolutely radiant during those four days. We had about 1,600 fans come out to watch the final match played between Ontario and Alberta.

It seemed to me that every girl there knew that they were a part of a new era. They were so appreciative of having the chance to participate not only in a hockey event but also a women's event. Often, in the hallways during the tournament, teams would go out to talk to other teams to learn more about each other's experiences playing the game. Those girls knew nothing like this had ever occurred before. It was beautiful to see so many powerful women coming together to create their own version of this important Canadian institution.

It was also fantastic that Shoppers specifically was able to come on board with our project because their main target audience was *women*. The deal worked well for both us and Shoppers, as the latter was in the process of marketing an active lifestyle to their female customers, and we needed a sponsor who was willing to support a bunch of "hockey misfits." The championship was a great way to use real athletes to promote this kind of a sporty image for women, which was a really new idea back then.

However, I did find it rather comical that three of their models from the 1970s, known as the "Shoppers Three," were brought in to attend one of our press conferences. There were very few women in hockey at the time who chose to adhere to the wispy, dainty 'feminine' image that these models stood for, which had been promoted largely as the bodily ideal in society during the years following the war. These girls stuck out like a sore thumb next to the rough and tough group of hockey-playing tomboys who had dismissed social customs to come play the game they loved at our tournament.

Nevertheless, I was very pleased that Shoppers was willing to begin a new era by promoting other kinds of role models for women to aspire to in the form of our beautiful female hockey players, as well as other amazing role models like Abby Hoffman and Maureen McTeer. We were also able to bring in Diane Jones Konihowski, a friend of Maureen's who was an Olympic Pentathlete, as well as the mother of "The Great One," Phyllis Gretzky, who dropped the puck at the opening ceremonies.

Aside from money, Shoppers Drug Mart supplied the jerseys for the event, which looked so sharp and professional that they nearly made me cry with joy when I unpacked them. Shoppers also gave us sports bags to be given out as awards to the players, such as for MVP, Top Scorer, and Best Goaltender. The girls from the winning team even got a loot bag full of Planters Peanuts and Shoppers Drug Mart beauty products from the *Bonne Belle* line, including shampoo, crème rinse, sanitary napkins, soap, body lotion, deodorant, and baby powder.

However, it was the sanitary napkins that had the biggest hit – and the result turned out to be quite entertaining! By the end of the day, those napkins were posted all over the tournament. They were stuck to walls, people, and more. I recall a moment of particular comedic value, where a goalie came out with a smattering of sanitary pads stuck to her goalie pads, and she was carrying a sign that read something along the lines of *"I'm always protected."* The girls were really having a good time with their joke!

At the end of the second last night, April 3, we held a banquet for the players at a hall next to the arena. We were overwhelmed – we had no idea how our financial situation would allow us to show our appreciation for sacrifices made by these women players who had gone to so much effort to make it to the tournament. We couldn't afford to hold them all in a hotel another night after the championship game had been played, so we had to host the banquet on the second last evening of the tournament, before any of the finals had even occurred!

We also didn't have awards or medals to give to every girl, but we were able to provide them with a nice meal – a roast beef dinner with mashed potatoes, salad, and wine and beer at an extra cost of $1.25 per drink. And yet no one was disorderly – the girls were respectful, and mostly just thrilled to be present.

We did have a talent show at the banquet, to spice things up a little. It was just for kicks, but it was really a great team building experience for many of the players. Every province had to put on a bit of a skit or a show. Some were good, and some were not, but all were fun nonetheless. We had teams who played guitar, sang, or just got up and bombed out laughing before they walked right back off the stage.

The girls were passionate about the sport, and very appreciative of the chance to play at a National Championship. It was so rewarding to see all the fun and excitement they brought to the event. That night was pivotal to the success of the tournament. That was when I became truly convinced that we had made our dream a reality: women's hockey was finally here to stay.

At this point, Murray Costello, the President of the CAHA, came up and said to me that we would never have been able to have this kind of entertainment at a male program. He was impressed by how the girls had taken ownership of the event. Here, the women had been able to step up and entertain themselves, whereas the men playing at a national level would most likely have taken for granted that they should have been *provided* with some kind of enjoyable diversion. I'm sure the girls would have loved to have such a perk themselves, but they realized that the money wasn't there – in this case, the girls were thankful to even have a championship!

We did some speeches at the banquet too, and told the players that they had been making history the past few days. This tournament was the stepping stone needed to someday see women's hockey make it to the Olympics. International women's hockey was everyone's long term goal, but we had to get the men's hockey programs on board in order to take it to the next level. I wanted women's hockey to be a separate program from the men, but with the same amount of funding, coverage, and opportunities for both divisions: two separate programs under one governing body. And although we have yet to achieve this true equality, we are much closer than when I was playing hockey as a young woman.

It was also at this event that Fran Rider told me that her Brampton organization was going to join the OWHA. I replied to her that we would be glad to sit down and discuss the transition. Soon after the Nationals, she became a member of the OWHA, quickly rose through the ranks, and went on to do wonders for the current women's hockey program in Canada. The first Women's Nationals gave Fran and her future colleagues the foundation they needed in order to take women's hockey to the international arena.

Organizing the first Women's National tournament was certainly no walk in the park – some weeks I recorded working over 80 hours total, and I actually became very sick after the second Women's Nationals in 1983 from the stress of trying to put the whole thing together – but I would do everything a thousand times over if I had to.

Looking back, my husband and a few others believe the odds of success were not in our favour, with so many hurdles in terms of budgets, timelines, discrimination, and bureaucratic chaos. Had I been set up to fail? If that had happened, women's hockey might have been dismissed as no more than the "ridiculous" idea that so many believed it was. However, I don't buy that interpretation. The set of challenges we were faced with was just a happenstance of time and place, although I do agree that there were certainly many who resisted the movement. Nonetheless, I'm thankful that we were able to provide a positive experience for so many women in the sport, and contribute to the growth of our national program.

Nowadays, the numbers in boys' minor hockey in Canada are actually dwindling because of all the other sport choices available, along with the fact that between equipment, icetime, and travel, hockey can be a very expensive game. Because of this demographic shift, Hockey Canada is currently pouring their support and resources into our women's program, where there is a renewed interest in the sport at the minor levels.

It is sweet victory for me to see our women's program growing, despite the difficulties still faces at the elite level. I am confident that despite the current setbacks, if women and their supporters can rise to the occasion and create real cultural and physical change in professional sports leagues and the society at large, there will be more opportunities for funding and recognition for girls in hockey in the future.

The Female Council

Another advancement in women's hockey to come out of this national event was the development of the *Female Council*, a group that still serves as the main voice for women's hockey in Canada.

Following a nationwide meeting on girls' hockey in January 1981 in Toronto that involved the CAHA, the OWHA, and other leaders in female hockey, it was decided that this new organization would be formed under the CAHA to represent the voices of all women in Canada's hockey world.

The CAHA already had a Minor Council, a Senior Council, and other groups that represented different demographics of the Canadian game. Before sanctioning our event, one of the CAHA's stipulations had been that we had to create a group like the Female Council to add to their ranks to represent the female population, and I thought a council like this was a wonderful idea that could really help girls advance in the sport.

However, how the CAHA set about creating this committee was especially interesting to me. The CAHA asked their male hockey representative in each province to personally choose a volunteer to sit on the new Female Council. While many of the individuals chosen were well-known to the women's hockey community in their area thanks to the many hours they had already devoted to helping their local girls' programs, there were a few names that none of us had ever heard before – and more often than not, these no-name representatives were men, with extremely little experience in women's hockey.

In some cases, these no-name men were likely chosen because of a lack of a strong woman's program in their province. However in a few cases, these individuals took the position away from more qualified people who were already highly involved in the women's program in their province – people who would have been in a better position to provide good advice to the council.

In the end, the original representatives chosen were Gertie Baron from Manitoba, Frank Champion Demers from Ontario (soon replaced by Fran Rider), Art Noseworthy from Quebec, Susan Dalziel from P.E.I., Vye Flindall from B.C., Howard Myatt from New Brunswick, Steve Saunders from Nova Scotia, Colleen Tapper from Newfoundland, Nancy Dragan from Saskatchewan, and Sue Sneft from Alberta.

We didn't include the Territories on the council, which I suppose is testament to the unfortunate and shameful disconnect that existed at that time between the colonial south and the more Indigenous northern communities in Canada. Nonetheless, uniting the provinces was a major achievement, although it certainly left room for future improvement.

Working alongside Nova Scotia representative Steve Saunders, I set about herding these 10 individuals together during the 1982 Nationals. The first meeting we called was held one day after the tournament, on April 5, 1982, and it was here that we stabilized the first official communication network between the girls' hockey associations of each province.

I was lucky enough to have been voted in as chairperson of this new Female Council at that first meeting, and subsequently, I earned a spot on the CAHA Board of Directors.

It was at this start-up meeting that we began to orchestrate the first ever national strategy for women's hockey in Canada and started building the foundation for the minor hockey infrastructure that young girls in the country enjoy today. We decided to focus our efforts on contributing to the development of the women's program through education at the coach, referee, fan, parent, and player levels, using clinics and seminars to help promote a positive image of the game in all demographics.

We had to present our strategy to the CAHA at their annual general meeting in Newfoundland in May of that same year. The Newfoundland meeting was a general meeting, which meant that *all* members of the various council subgroups could attend, not just the CAHA executive board, so I attended meetings there for both the Female Council and the Board of Directors.

My trip to Newfoundland turned out to be quite an unforgettable weekend. For starters, I had to go through the whole thing in a walking cast, because I'd done a terrific job on my ankle a

135

few weeks earlier. I'd been chumming around with my boyfriend Al and received a hipcheck that sent me stumbling over the curb of a sidewalk, where I did a pretty good job at twisting my foot and breaking the bone!

However, because I was working for the HODC at the time, I actually had the privilege of being treated by the doctors for the Toronto Maple Leafs, who were affiliated with my organization. I remember my jaw almost dropped when I heard one doctor say that he didn't think the bones and ligaments "needed surgery," because up until that point, I hadn't even known surgery was in question!

In the long run, my boot cast didn't matter much – Newfoundland was a hoot whether I had to get around on crutches or not! The first night we arrived, we had a big group get-together and enjoyed watching the locals perform some lovely music with a strong Maritime flare. It was a regular Gumboot Cloggeroo! There were men and women singing and playing guitars who looked like they'd walked right off a fishing boat – and I think a lot of them really had!

About halfway through the night, we had to get what the locals call "Screeched-In," which is a ceremony to welcome "Mainlanders" to their province. The ceremony involves drinking a shot of Screech, a local hard rum, and then reciting a funny little poem. If you can't recite the poem, however, then you have to kiss a cod! We all had a lot of laughs that evening, despite some of us having to pucker up to a fish!

The next morning, it was back to board meetings, with our feet dragging a little more than usual. Nonetheless, some really good discussions came out of that weekend. One was with the Female Council, only our second meeting ever. We talked a lot more about the growth of the women's game, and about what role we should play in its evolution. This was the first time we, as an organization, were really representing women's hockey in Canada.

One of the first topics we debated was what we should name ourselves. Rider and a few others wanted to call it the *Women's* Council, but I thought the *Female* Council would be more appropriate. Although at that time the majority of players affiliated with the OWHA were mature women, I pushed to have the young girls' programs put at the forefront of our priorities because those girls were our future. We needed kids to register with our program if we wanted to see women's hockey still being played in 10, 20, or even 50 years, and we had to have a name that was welcoming, inclusive and reflected this development-oriented position.

We also talked about implementing some national leadership camps for young women in hockey in order to give our top-tier athletes the chance to make greater progress in their sport, and to spread what they learned with others. We hoped they would continue to be positive role models for the youth of the country, to help inspire more girls to take up the hockey stick torch and carry on playing the game we loved.

We held the first of these camps at York University in July of 1982. We picked up about 20 elite U-18 girls up from the Pearson airport and drove them to the campus where they'd be staying in the dorms and getting complimentary meals from the dining hall.

These girls benefitted, of course, from on and off-ice training sessions to help them play smarter, faster, and stronger (as well as some scrimmages and baseball just for fun). But we also had them all become certified NCCP (National Coaching Certification Program) Level 2 Coaches and official Level 1 Referees, in the hope that they could return to their home provinces and use these skills to contribute to the growth and development of their own local girls' hockey programs.

These camps were not the only great advances to come out of the Newfoundland meeting. While out east, we also talked about how to improve on the women's Nationals – because all of the sudden, the Nationals were no longer a Rhonda or an OWHA responsibility, but a Female Council or CAHA one! And what a relief it was to have that load off my shoulders!

We were lucky enough to have the CAHA President Murray Costello on our side as a supporter of the women's program. Murray was a lawyer, so he understood contemporary views about political correctness and human rights, and knew he had to help our program if he could. He made a point of attending all of the games at the first Women's Nationals.

However, what Murray ordained officially, and what actually happened, were two *very* different things. We still had some trouble getting a lot of the "die hards" to accept having women's programs blossom alongside the men's programs – and an added challenge was that sometimes these "die hards" were high up in hockey administration.

XI

1982 –

A Woman in the CAHA

My involvement as a woman with the Canadian Amateur Hockey Association began early. In the very beginning, right after the first Nationals, the CAHA nominated me to sit on the board for the National Development Committee, which was similar to the HODC except that it focused on the development of elite programs in Canada. But I had a hard time committing myself to work with this program because although it was undoubtedly a necessary piece of Canadian hockey infrastructure, it had absolutely nothing to do with women at that point!

Moreover, I hadn't finished my contract with the HODC and I was still working with the OWHA, so I really didn't have the time to take on another big job like this one. There simply weren't enough hours in a day. It was a nice gesture that the CAHA was trying to integrate women into their organization, but I turned it down, because if I was going to be there at all, I was going to work on something that would help other women in the sport!

Thankfully, in May of 1982, just two months after being voted Director of the Female Council, I had the "privilege" of being the first woman to sit on the Canadian Amateur Hockey Association's Board of Directors, the only one in all the 65 years they had been around! 51

I think this position was one of the most important advances we had ever made in women's hockey. For once, women were getting a say in the development of the game at a higher level. The only step up from there would have been to grab a seat for ourselves on the governing board of the NHL – a jump which a handful of women have finally made today!52

In some respects, I believe that we have also fallen backwards since the 1980s, away from my dream of equal parallel programs for both sexes at all levels. When the CAHA underwent a structural reorganization many years after my time as Director, they dropped the head of the Female Council from their executive board. Consequently, the CAHA Board of Directors no longer has any females eligible to vote within their ranks.53

Moreover, as I'm sure it is for the few women on the NHL Board of Governors today, my involvement with the Canadian Board

---

51 Sadly, this position was revoked a few years after my era, and the Female Council now sits as a subgroup of Hockey Canada, not as an equal voice in their administration.
52 However, only 5 out of 127 individuals currently sitting on the NHL Board of Governors are women – a paltry representation of only 3.93%, but still progress!
53 Take a look at this striking picture of the current Hockey Canada Board of Directors: https://www.hockeycanada.ca/en-ca/corporate/about/board-of-directors; Adams, Carly, and Julie Stevens. "Change and grassroots movement: re-conceptiualizing women's hockey governance in Canada," *Int. J. Sport Management and Merketing,* Vol. 2, No. 4, p. 361;

of Directors was certainly no day at the beach. Life was not easy for a woman in the CAHA. Thanks to the Nationals, we had made enough progress to have our sport become acceptable for girls to play, but we had by no means eradicated the gender inequality that was still prevalent in society at large. We'd merely chipped the tooth of the beast.

I recall an incident I had with a member of the Hockey Ontario Development Committee during my inaugural days on the CAHA that speaks well to how the integration of women was received in these kinds of more powerful (male) sport associations.

I had gone out to lunch one day and left my office at the HODC headquarters unattended. When I came back, I discovered that this man, my colleague, had taken a knitted doll that I'd had as adornment at my desk and hung it by its neck with a makeshift noose above my workspace. Even if he passed it off as another "joke," the message was pretty clear: like the doll, the female sex was clearly not welcome in the male domain into which I was encroaching.

This doll was given to me by a dear friend who had passed away, and so it had particular sentimental value to me. The man who had hung my doll had proceeded to run around the office like a little boy, telling all his friends about the prank he'd just pulled on me. He thought himself quite the clown. In hindsight, I tend to agree – the only thing the fool was missing in that moment was a dunce cap.

I think my colleagues were in a bit of a jealous tizzy at all the new and exciting growth we were producing in the women's program. But the very fact that someone could make a joke about killing women to get them off the men's turf shows the extent to which the sexism entrenched in our culture was unnervingly flagrant. More importantly, this chauvinism wasn't only present on an individual level. It still remains fixed in the system as much as in personal interactions.

I can picture a similarly sickening incident that occurred at the Royal York Hotel in Toronto at one of my first meetings with the CAHA. After checking in, I was being escorted to check into my room, which was across the hall from a few of my fellow board members' rooms. The other board members had already checked in and were in their rooms having a few drinks after their day of travel. Well, wasn't everyone surprised when, upon entering my room with the bellboy, we discovered a man lying face down on the bed, completely unconscious.

I don't know what became of the unconscious man, whether he was alright after he was taken away in the ambulance or not, but you can imagine the flood of comments my colleagues on the board started spewing after they saw the incident that had just occurred.

They made it out like I was some kind of brutal man-hater – *"Don't mess with Rhonda,"* or *"Look at what happened to the last man she dealt with,"* and the like. And I was just the unlucky one to have been assigned to that hotel room – I had never even met the poor man in my life.

Again, the comments proffered by my male peers were supposedly all "jokes," but that doesn't take away from the fact that they still stung me inside. It was already bad enough that I was the only young woman on a board full of old men, but here they were making hurtful and unnecessary remarks at one of my very first meetings on the job.

It should also be mentioned that even though I had this "equal" position on the CAHA Board of Directors, I didn't initially have a vote on the council like the other (male) members. It went without saying that all members of the board were supposed to have a vote, but I had been denied this right on the basis of being involved in the women's program, which to them wasn't worthy of a vote because it was still so new and less developed. They seemed to have a whole lot of trouble figuring out exactly how the woman's game could fit into the parameters of their previously all-male hockey program, when to us the answer was very clear – treat us as equals.

Naturally, the Female Council wanted the right to add our two cents and cast a ballot for decisions that often directly affected women's hockey. After all, my position on the board was relatively useless without a vote. So we sent a letter to President Murray Costello and asked him about giving women an equal voice on the council. Murray agreed that it was something that needed to happen, and told me he would add it as a topic for discussion at the next meeting (which happened to be the weekend when I found the unconscious man in my hotel room at the Royal York in Toronto).

However, a few of the other members were not quite as receptive to the idea of giving me a vote. In fact, one man, who for privacy's sake we will call "Barry," who was a senior CAHA executive at the time acted downright hostile towards me.

Going into the meeting, I remember Barry kept on approaching me in the hallway, and *telling* me that the women didn't want a vote, because for some reason he had it stuck in his head that we shouldn't have one, and he wanted me to agree with him.

Perhaps it was my own fault that he thought this way, because all the times he came up to me before the meeting insinuating that I should be happy with not having a vote, I had quietly avoided giving him a direct answer about whether or not I agreed, because I knew he wasn't going to like what I said, and I was afraid of having a fight with him in the lobby of the hotel where our words weren't officially recorded by a secretary.

It turned out that it didn't matter much whether or not the fight was recorded – that factor certainly didn't seem to deter Barry from raising his voice at me, as if chastising a child, in front of the entire panel of 20 or so directors when I asked for a vote during the meeting.

Barry called me a liar, said I'd never wanted the vote, and positively yelled from across the table that "the women's program wasn't developed enough to warrant a vote," that we "didn't *need* one," and then finished off by shouting some insulting personal comments that were so mean they almost brought me to tears. The man was absolutely irate, and I found the whole situation to be remarkably intimidating.

Meeting protocol had it that all speakers stood when they talked, so it was just the two of us standing up, the focus of every other member's attention, with me at the bottom of the U-shaped panel, and Barry in his position with the other executives at the head of the room, all his wrath absolutely raining down on me.

Barry's anger stemmed partly from discrimination and partly from politics. As an employee of the HODC, there were many on the board (like Barry) who didn't think that I should get a vote because of their personal affiliations with the HODC which was a competitor of the Ontario Hockey Association (for boys). I tried to stand my ground through the barrage of insults and remind Barry that I was here to talk about getting a vote for the women, and not about his petty hockey politics.

However, I'm sure he would not have been quite as cantankerous if the issue had been strictly political. Most of the CAHA was walking on eggshells at that time, because they knew Sport Canada wanted them to adopt women's hockey and, as one of their main sources of funding, they had to listen to Abby Hoffman and make room for our program whether they liked it or not.[54] I'm sure a decision such as this (going against the era's cultural norms) got on the nerves many of the men in that meeting room, although Barry was the only one to start hollering about it.

Murray called a brief break after Barry's tantrum to try to cool things down a little and see if Barry's face could lose a shade or two of red before we continued with the meeting. I don't know what my face looked like at that time, but I knew the rest of me was shaking. I

---

[54] It's crazy to think that Abby Hoffman and her colleagues at Sport Canada had so easily brought one of the most powerful sport organizations in Canada to their knees! Go Abby!

was proud of myself for having stood up to the man, but I was still a little traumatized by what had just occurred.

As I got up to leave for the break, another male representative from PEI came up to me and told me that he had nearly joined in Barry's fight himself, as if to tell me that he felt the same as Barry, and that I was lucky that he hadn't started yelling at me as well. I don't understand why he even felt the need to make such a comment, especially when it was clear his colleague had already done a sufficient job in stating his opinions. It certainly didn't make me feel any better about humanity.

Nonetheless, when we returned from the meeting after Barry calmed down, Murray had us cast our vote despite the protests, and thankfully the decision came out with the majority of ballots cast in my favour. When everything was finally finished, Murray Costello came up to me and said something along the lines of "Rhonda, the history books are never going to believe what went down today." He was as appalled as I was at the odious behaviour of some of his board members. Barry was never promoted to the position of President, and I would bet that the reasoning behind this was crystal clear – his extreme unprofessionalism at this meeting and others were more than enough to keep him from the big chair.

Those few short weeks before and after the first Women's Nationals seemed to have no end of surprises in store for me – some rewarding and others challenging. It is a wonder that we could have packed so much turmoil and energy into such a short amount of time – a fact which to me is one of the most incredible parts of these early days of the women's hockey program. Quite literally, we went from almost nothing to having a national governing body for the sport in under three months – although this certainly didn't come without a lot of hard work!

Sadly, the end of these golden days for me was drawing near. Little did I know how deeply some of the challenges that had occurred in those three months could affect the future of my career in women's hockey, and not in a positive fashion.

Me Too

I had a very unfortunate encounter with a man I was working with leading up to the first Women's Nationals in 1982.

Before the incident, I had been close with this man. We had worked side by side for a few years, during which time he contributed laudable efforts to the women's program in Canada. I would say I fully trusted him, and had a lot of respect for both him and his work.

All that changed in March of 1982. I had been working on some spreadsheets and info graphics for the Nationals, and I'd asked this individual to give me his opinion on one of the sheets. The OWHA had been staying at the Talisman Hotel in Ottawa and in order to save some money, the members decided to hold all our meetings in our personal rooms as opposed to wasting money renting a board room.

For this reason, it was just me and the man alone in the room, and I had spread out all the papers on the hotel bed, for lack of a better desk. I never thought anything of inviting him into my room to take a look at the documents, since we'd had professional meetings like this many times before, plus I'd left the hotel door open. Moreover, I knew his wife well. I had visited with them at their lovely home, and I thought the world of both of them.

We were about halfway through the conversation when this man turned to me and said, "Rhonda, you know, I wouldn't be disappointed if you came onto me right now."

I was so taken aback that I just stopped for a moment, and then started laughing. There was absolutely no way in hell that I was going to sleep with this man! He was like an uncle to me. And he had a wife!

But after a few seconds, when I looked at his face, I knew he hadn't been joking. What's more, I saw that my naive laughter at the proposition had hurt his pride. The man was no longer my ally.

I'm lucky that I wasn't physically hurt in that moment, like so many women who have stood in that same kind of place before and after me – thankfully this isn't that kind of story. My colleague and I both recognized that the conversation was very clearly finished, and he left the room without saying another word.

I stood there for a moment, still processing what had just occurred. On its own, the incident wasn't horrible – uncomfortable, yes, and certainly not *alright*, but something I could handle. However, I wasn't prepared for the fallout of this moment – that was what really changed my life.

I had to keep working with this man if I wanted to see the Women's Nationals up and running, so I shut my mouth and carried on as though nothing had happened. Evidently, I no longer had the same agreeable relationship with the man after that day in March. His attitude toward me changed entirely, and he became surly and quarrelsome with me from that point forward.

This man was my superior in the business side of the sport, and an original member of the Female Council. However, after the first meeting, he removed himself from the Female Council and parachuted in Fran Rider to take his place without a vote from the other members. He was making every effort to avoid contact with me if he could.

I'll admit that I had watched on in slight disbelief as only a few months prior to my incident, this same man had handed plaques to a few long-standing board members, thanking them for their service and wishing them a nice life as he swept them out the door of the organization. I'd trusted him as my superior, so I had foolishly assumed that he had his reasons and that they must be good ones.

With this and my incident in mind, I was hardly surprised when he started doing the same sort of sweeping to me, although I'm sure his reasons were a little different this time. When I was elected President of the Female Council, he turned around in the first meeting (the only one he attended), and voiced his concern to the other members that they had made a "bad" decision, that I wasn't the right fit for the job – an abrupt change of opinion considering he had been fully supporting me throughout the Women's Nationals and had even once *promoted* me to become VP of the OWHA!

The other council members kindly ignored his recommendations and kept me in the position under the assumption that I was best suited to chair the group since I had just organized a National tournament for women in the country and knew a lot about the state of girls' hockey all over. But he didn't seem to agree.

It was after this meeting that the real effects of the incident began to show. This man, my superior, waited until everyone had left the boardroom that day, then came over to me once again as I was packing up my things. He looked me in the eyes and told me: "You do not have a future in women's ice hockey." He then followed through on that promise.

My footholds in the hockey world began to unravel quickly after that. I sat as chair of the second Women's Nationals again in 1983, but after my contract ended with the HODC in 1984, it was not renewed. The same year, the OWHA "discontinued their affiliation" with me, meaning that I was also no longer eligible to be a member of the Female Council or the CAHA.

This effectively ended my career in women's hockey development and administration, although I tried to remain an active volunteer in hockey in other ways. I became an NCCP instructor and worked from 1984 to 1992 with the OMHA (the Ontario [boys] Minor Hockey Association) and the MTHL (Metro Toronto [boys] Hockey League) teaching coaching clinics and certification classes, the only woman in the program at the time.

At that time, I was living in Bolton with my husband Al, and because this area was growing so fast, Al and I spent all of our weekends certifying new coaches in the York and Peel Regions. We must have certified a few thousand coaches in those eight years. In fact, Spike McConnell, our program director, was so pleased with our output that he invited the two of us to work as technical advisors in player skill analysis for the under-17 elite Olympic prospect program (and again, I was the only woman there).

I tried to get my Level 4 Coaching Certification during this period. I enrolled in a class in Ottawa (once more the only woman there), did all the tests and assignments, attended all the sessions – but still didn't come out with a credit like all the rest of my (male) peers. The man instructing the course, a retired air force general, seemed to think that it was okay to create his own rules and standards for the program, and evidently, I didn't fit the broad-shouldered mould he was looking for.

I also volunteered with the Queen's University alumni ice hockey association and with the Kingston Kodiak Girls' Hockey Association when I could. I helped run a few Outward Bound sessions as well, which were leadership workshops for young girls who played team sports.

In terms of career changes, I ended up in the business sector – in Human Resources, where I eventually opened my own firm, RET Staffing Services, and sold it to Olsten (now Adecco) in 1993.

During all these years, I watched in wonder as Fran Rider rose to become President of the OWHA, and started making powerful advances for women in sport. Fran quickly became a dominant force in the world of women's hockey, and strongly influenced the shape of the program. This is perhaps why an Ontario rep has never held the Presidency on the Female Council after me, because our province would have held a monopoly on all the others if we were to hold the reins of the Female Council and also have Fran at the helm of the OWHA!

The position of OWHA President was initially a volunteer position, but it became a salaried one sometime after Fran came on board. This was possible because after the women's program had affiliated with the CAHA, the OWHA started processing all the registration money and mandatory CAHA $1 insurance fees, meaning the cash flowing through our organization was enough to use as a payroll for the President.

Fran has done some wonderful things with her OWHA Presidency, which she still holds with an iron grip some three decades later. One of her major accomplishments was getting the women's game to the international arena, a project which I could only dream of at that point. It really is ludicrous when you think about it – I was there and more than willing to help the women's program in any way I could, and yet I had been successfully ousted and kept from contributing to the OWHA because I had rejected the unwanted advances of my superior.

I carried the secret of that hotel meeting on my back for years, believing that I had no right to complain – after all, I had invited that man into my room, and so I'd believed the error was on me. It took until I was about 65 before I had an "*ahah!*" moment during the #MeToo movement and realized that I had done absolutely nothing wrong. Inviting a man to look at spreadsheets and refusing to sleep with him is under no circumstance a valid excuse to be forcibly kept from participating in a career, or more importantly, a passion.

I know this type of abuse of authority is not uncommon in sports and administration positions, and still occurs today. I am definitely not the only woman to have suffered through this kind of humiliation or frustration – and so many of our sisters still need help. We need to stand up, be loud, and make our voices heard – things I wish I had known in 1982.

XIII

Cutting Out the Contact

I think it is important to pause from the story here and talk about one last key episode of my time in women's hockey administration before I was given the boot – an episode that concerns the instigation of non-contact legislation for girls.

As I mentioned before, until the first Nationals, women's hockey was composed of a ragtag series of leagues and teams with different sets of rules regarding body contact in games – some had no contact at all, some had full contact, some had hip-checks only, and some had even banned slapshots.

A lot of the time, these rules stemmed from local customs that had remained unchanged since before the 1940s via the small pockets of women's hockey that survived the post-war period. Other times, the contact had been removed in the new leagues that sprang up in the 1960s, again because of the ridiculous notion that women were more vulnerable or delicate than our brothers.

Evidently, this reasoning was absurd – we were no more likely to be injured by contact than men. However, I am not stating here that I think all women should have been playing contact hockey – quite the opposite in fact.

It must be understood that non-contact play is by no means a sign of female weakness; rather, it is a good safety practice for men and women alike. Hockey is a dangerous sport – we're out there on literal *blades*, wearing rock-solid equipment, and skating very fast while carrying a lot of weight behind us; it is no wonder that so many players sustain injuries such as bruises, cuts, broken bones, sprained joints, and worst of all, concussions.

Brain trauma is a very serious issue that individuals in high-level leagues like the NHL are only just beginning to open up about. However there are a substantial number of players at all levels who have had to deal with the serious health repercussions of enduring hits leading to life-impairing concussions. And the more contact allowed in a game, the greater the chances that a player is going to be injured.

Recall that when a cohesive set of regulations was put in place for women's hockey across the country at the first Women's Nationals, we had to adopt the CAHA rules in order to gain their support and sanctioning. This meant the games were full-contact, a format which worked just the same for women as it did the men – although whether we can qualify this system as "good" is another question entirely.

To add to the danger factor, it was difficult to promote a contact league for women at the first Nationals in a culture where there were still such strong stereotypes about women being the "fragile" sex. A lot of parents, and even young girls themselves, were not attracted to playing a game that they believed could hurt them due to their female "vulnerability." Essentially, the rough games televised at the first Nationals were hindering us from fulfilling our goal of using elite athletes to promote hockey in the younger demographic – a strategy which was necessary to ensure the survival of the sport for girls in the future.

I started pushing to have the contact taken out of the girls' game at that famous general meeting in Newfoundland, although some provinces had already started the discussion about removing contact for all sanctioned women's leagues in Canada at the first Nationals.

As the product of the Ontarian system where girls played non-contact hockey in University and contact hockey in women's community leagues, I had the chance to dabble in both varieties of the sport and consider the pros and cons of each.

Reflecting on all my years of playing, I eventually came up with four good reasons as to why removing contact would help advance the women's game:

- Firstly, removing all contact would unify the playing regulations across the country, creating less confusion for inter-league games and tournaments.

- Secondly, it would put the focus of the game back onto the skill and fitness involved (instead of who could hurt their opponents the most), meaning the game would be won by the most *capable* team, and not by the one most violent or intimidating one.

- Thirdly, as already mentioned, removing contact would decrease injury rates, making a safer game for all involved.

- And finally, it would allow us to promote the game to young kids whose parents were still caught up in the idea that their 10-year-old daughters were somehow not as strong as their 10-year-old sons. Moreover, it would ensure that even in small towns where there was only one women's team with a wide range of ages, the kids age 9 or 10 would be more inclined to play a game if they weren't frightened by the prospect of being hit by a woman who was twice their age and a good 30 to 50 pounds heavier!

For these reasons, I lobbied at the CAHA and Female Council levels to try and convince my peers that we really needed to cut the contact out of our games. I called the female reps from British Columbia, Alberta, New Brunswick, Quebec and PEI to try and convince them of the importance of removing contact from the women's game and was well received. Mind you, I knew I was running a fairly high risk in doing this because I was going against the wishes of my home province, which had (and still has) representatives adamantly opposed to the idea.

After much discussion and debate, I pushed my colleagues on the Female Council to hold a vote on the subject in the spring of

1983, and thankfully, nine out of 10 representatives voted to have the contact removed. [55] This meant that all sanctioned national tournaments in Canada were henceforth contact-free, just in time for the second Women's Nationals in April of 1983.

The removal of contact from girls' sports would soon be adopted by a few provinces in Canada and spread to groups in other countries like the AHAUS (Amateur Hockey Association of the United States, now USA Hockey) by 1985. It would eventually become the international standard when it was used in the second global women's tournament run by the IIHF (International Ice Hockey Federation) in 1994. Mind you, it was only after this international adoption that the rest of our Canadian provinces would finally come around to cutting the contact out of their games.

Moreover, our theory about the better reception of a safer sport proved correct – the registration numbers for girls in a program skyrocketed when bodychecking was removed. For example, after the second Women's Nationals in 1983, the registration numbers jumped from 5,379 girls to 9,074 girls by 1989. However, registration for girls in Canada actually dropped from 9,074 to only 8,164 after the first IIHF Women's World Championship in 1990, which were played with contact! Thankfully, the numbers would again rise significantly after the next international championship in 1992 provided strong female role models in a non-contact sport. [56]

[55] The only one to vote against the motion was my own Ontario representative!
[56] Hunter, Andria. "Hockey Registration in Canada." The Women's Hockey Web, www.whockey.com/country/canada/registration.html. Accessed 29 June 2019.

It is also important to note that we made the decision to remove contact in the hope that the women's program, so plastic in its infancy, could be moulded to set an example for a safer, less injury-prone game for *everyone,* boys included.

As the McMurtry Report had proven in 1974, the violence in (men's) hockey in the 1970s and '80s was rampant, and a lot of that had to do with the checking permitted in games. One of the later outcomes of the McMurtry Report and the work done by my peers on the HODC was that boys' hockey eventually followed in the footsteps of the girls' – contact was removed from some of their leagues, although mostly only for the younger age groups in the Canadian boys' minor hockey programs.

In the past few years there has been increasing pressure on Hockey Canada and the NHL to eliminate checking from the game altogether. This has resulted in recent changes to boys' minor hockey; for example, in 2013 the Hockey Canada ban on checking was recently pushed back to include the Peewee age group (11-12-year-olds). Yet despite these advances, we are still a long way from convincing the NHL that the health risk their players are continuously running is quite severe, and in no way worth the money they make by selling this violence to the media. Too many players have incurred serious irreparable brain damage because of concussions sustained in our sport. There are some who have even died from this repeated cerebral trauma.

Carl Noble and many others have confided to me that they prefer to watch women's games these days because they're of a much higher calibre in terms of skill level compared to men's games, which are still filled with goons, fights and big hits – or as Carl calls it, "garbage."

I believe that contributing to the removal of contact from the women's game was the most important thing I did in all my years in the women's program. Not only did it allow the program to grow, but it also helped to make it a safer pastime for everyone impacted. I am so thankful that I was able to push past the challenges I faced after the first Women's Nationals and score that last goal before my days in hockey administration came to an involuntary close.

Women's Hockey
In the International Arena

Whether I was involved at the time or not, the 1980s and '90s were an exciting period for women in ice hockey. With a solid national infrastructure to build upon, Fran Rider and her team worked very hard to coordinate with other countries and come up with an official international tournament for women in the sport.

A series of trans-continental games took place just a few years after the first Nationals that allowed Canadian women to get a feel for the quality of play in other countries, and vice versa. Canada and the United States had long been playing each other in exhibition games, and we'd even had unofficial "North American" championships like the Wallaceburg Lipstick Tournament in the 1960s and '70s. The difference now was that girls' teams such as those in Huntsville and Mississauga were beginning to venture out across the pond to compete against their European neighbours.

Al and I volunteered as extra hands to help out with one of the first team exchanges in 1982, which involved the Huntsville Honeys and their billets from Denmark. What a fun few weeks that turned out to be! We drove down to meet the Danish "RIK" (Rungsted Ishockey Klub) team at Toronto's Pearson Airport in my original-model Subaru and Al's Dodge pickup truck, and we got special treatment by the airport traffic controllers who asked us to drive the wrong way down a one-way road just to get to the RIK team – they wanted to keep Terminal 1 from grinding to a halt thanks to all the players' bags and equipment!

From there, we drove everyone over to a welcoming party at a condo downtown where we gave them snacks and special Canadian and Huntsville Honey pins (see Appendix E). Later that weekend, Al ran a free power skating clinic to further welcome our new European friends.[57]

The Danish girls were hosted by the Toronto Aeros and later the Huntsville Honeys in a billeting system, so we lodged our travellers with the families of their host teams. This was a lovely opportunity to have some cross-cultural exchanges and increase the global awareness of both our players and theirs!

A few comical situations arose out of these billet stays. One was when a Danish player emerged from the bathroom after a shower at one of her hosts' houses to ask for a towel, dressed only in her bra and panties. Her hosts were absolutely floored! Why, in those days in Canada, it was considered unacceptable to even have your bra strap showing! Yet here were girls with European customs who didn't think

[57] Al and I were engaged at that time, to be married in the winter of 1983. A lot of our "date nights" like this had a strong hockey focus, because that was our mutual passion!

anything of coming out half naked! I daresay it was a good way to expand our North American mindsets on the topic of sexist dress codes and the liberalization of male societal control on the female body.

Thankfully, the billeting system was a very laid back and unofficial way to host our exchange partners, so this little hiccup didn't cause any major problems and the rest of their trip ran smoothly. After a successful two weeks of tourism and evenly-matched games against a handful of different Ontarian teams, the Danish girls waved goodbye and returned home to await the Honeys' arrival in Denmark the next year to complete the exchange.

Neither Al nor I took part in the trip to Denmark with the Honeys, but from the stories that came back it sounded like the girls all had a very good time. Gail Cummings, the little girl who had been kicked off a boys' team 10 years after Abby Hoffman, had finally found herself a hockey home in the Honeys and was actually part of the group that travelled to Denmark. Gail scored multiple game-winning goals and became one of the team's star forward players. It is such a shame that the young boys' team who had refused her entry couldn't profit from Gail's incredible skill, but what a boon it was for the Honeys to have this strong young woman on their bench!

As is to be expected, the Honeys had to do a lot of fundraising to find the resources to cover the cost of the trip. Thankfully, they managed to acquire the financial assistance they needed with the help of Don and Joy Brandt from Brandt's Flowers. As a sweet gesture, the

Brandts even sent all the players some blossoms upon their arrival in Denmark to wish them luck in their games![58]

This kind of support was a welcome change in the system, but the best support of the trip was yet to come. When the girls returned from Denmark, they reported with delight how well they had been received by the public in Europe. The Danish people were well aware of the Canadian hockey team's arrival – our girls were taken aback to have multiple individuals come up to them on the street and welcome them to the country, or wish them luck in their games. The media coverage their trip received was extraordinary – far superior to any coverage that a girls' team had ever received in Canada.[59] Even upon their return to Canada, the Honeys were well-received in their hometown, where they were paraded around on firetrucks to celebrate their victories in Europe!

A similarly well-received exchange occurred just a few years later, when a girls' team from Mississauga coached by Joe Primeau Jr. (son of Joe Primeau the Leafs player) headed off to Finland. One of my old hockey peers, Joey Bush, recounted to me the story of the trip. Joey had never been to Finland and didn't speak the language, but she was chosen by her teammates to go over as a representative a few weeks early to set up accommodations, transportation and a playing schedule. Without internet, that was really the best way to do it back then!

[58] McConnell, Wendy. "Honeys work and effort pay off in Denmark." *The Forester* [Huntsville], 9 Mar. 1983.
[59] Ibid.

Joey returned to Finland a few weeks later with her team and played against a few different teams in Finland. The first was against a local girls' team, and it was evident by the beginning of the first game that the Finland girls were no match for our more developed Canadian team quite yet.

The Mississauga team was beating them horribly, so as per Canadian customs, Joey and her friends decided to stop scoring on their opponents out of politeness and sportsmanship. But when the Finland girls clued in to what Canada was doing, they came up to our girls and begged them to keep on playing to the best of their abilities, because the Finland team wanted to see an example of high-quality girls' hockey that they could strive towards!

In the second half of the trip, the Mississauga girls even lined up to try their hand against a Junior A boys' team. The stands were absolutely jam packed with hundreds of cheering people that night – Joey recalls that there were reporters in the lobby taking their pictures and people asking for autographs. The girls were really being treated like pros!

During the game itself, the two teams weren't allowed to hit or take slap shots – only a little bit of hip checking was permitted. The Finnish boys soon realized that this was a game they weren't going to win playing with their left hands – they had met a set of equal rivals. The fans were amazed by the phenomenal skill level of the Mississauga team and were going wild up in the stands as our girls started scoring goals on their Junior A opponents. However, according to Joey, a lot of the boys were becoming a little cross and choleric after they realized with a shock that they were in danger of losing to the women. To keep the penalties in check, the refs decided to call the game early while the score was tied between the two teams.

Exciting hockey exchanges like this were only the beginning of the international women's hockey community that was beginning to develop in the early '80s and '90s. Fran Rider's hand was already steadily guiding a significant portion of the women's hockey program in Canada by the end of the 1980s, but soon her influence would spread to an international level as she and her team organized the very first Women's World Championship held in Ottawa, Ontario in 1990. After that, they helped to see the game make its way into the 1998 Olympics in Nagano, Japan. Thanks to these advances, the registration numbers for female players in Canada have continued to grow over the years, with a total of 88,541 female players registered under Hockey Canada in the 2016-17 season.[60]

By 1994, I was living with Al back in the Kingston area. I was inducted into the Kingston Sports Hall of Fame in 1997, and I spent my time kayaking and working in the HR business sector. I had resigned myself to enjoying the progress in the sport on television and playing hockey recreationally in my women's league in Kingston.

I was content. Life was good. But hockey wasn't done dealing out the surprises it had in store for me.

[60] "Hockey Canada Annual Report." *Hockey Canada*, June 2017, cdn.hockeycanada.ca/hockeycanada/Corporate/About/Downloads/2016-17-annual-report-e.pdf. Accessed 29 June 2019.

Injury and Lawsuit

It was a cold day on January 24, 2004. I laced up my skates as per routine and headed onto the ice to play the game I loved in my old girls' league in Kingston. I was 50 years old.

Even at 50, I was in really good shape – I had completed three sprint triathlons the previous summer and I'd spent many of the warmer evenings kayaking out on the back lakes near the beautiful house I shared with Al in Verona, a small town near my home city. In the winter, I was kept busy playing in my "ladies'" league five times a week. I was also working full time in HR and making about $65,000 a year.

On the ice that day, the game was going well. We were playing a strong team and the score was 6 -1 in favour of our opponents, but I was still having a grand old time skating my heart out as usual.

Women's recreational hockey is a peculiar beast. Due to the relatively new resurgence of the women's game, the player profiles involved in women's rec hockey come from diverse backgrounds

168

with highly different skill levels. Unlike in the men's rec sport, a study done in 2012 by Norm O'Reilly and Denyse Lafrance Horning found that for women, "Hockey experience varied significantly as some were novice players participating in their very first season of play, and others reportedly had played for as long as forty-five years."[61]

I believe this factor makes women's recreational leagues particularly dangerous, as the varying skating speeds and levels of aggression do not always match the overall quality of play, creating extensive room for collision and injury.

I hope that as the next generation of female rec players come through the system, they will not experience this issue since the majority of women will have gained experience playing throughout their youth. However, since this was not yet the case in 2004, I believe this player diversity may have contributed to the mishap I experienced on that fateful day in January.

As the end of the game drew near, I snagged up a pass from my winger and picked up some speed as I crossed the blue line with a clear shot on net. I headed towards the net and snap-shot the puck up into the mesh, scoring a goal before the opposing defenceman could stop me.

I didn't know that would be the last goal I ever scored.

[61] Lafrance Horning, Denyse. "Women's Recreational Hockey: A New Player Profile," in Ellison, Jenny, and Jennifer Anderson, editors. *Hockey : Challenging Canada's Game, Au-Delà Du Sport National.* Canadian Museum of History, 2018, p. 169. *Project Muse*, https://muse-jhu-edu.proxy3.library.mcgill.ca/chapter/2109396. Accessed 13 Sept. 2019.

Before I knew what was happening, I collided with a player from the other team who had tried to stop me. The impact of the contact with the other player was mostly on the lower half of my body, so it sent me flying through the air and into the boards behind the net, head-first.

I don't think my opponent realized how fast I'd been skating. She'd badly misjudged her defensive move. I know she wasn't trying to send me into the boards – she only wanted to stop me from scoring and I'm sure she would never have even come near me if she knew what that collision would end up costing the both of us.

After I hit the boards, I remember there were people standing over me on the ice, trying to talk to me, but I couldn't hear them very well and I couldn't reply at all.

I knew I'd rung my bell pretty good, but after a few minutes I managed to get up and skate back to the bench. We were really short players that game and the last period was nearly over, so after I took a bit of a break and recovered from my confusion, I gritted my teeth through my headache and stepped back on the ice to help my team finish the game.

Two days later, my head was still throbbing, and I'd started having pain in my arms, hips and back. I went to the Hotel Dieu hospital in Kingston and was diagnosed with muscle damage, and then with a concussion after I saw a physiotherapist a few days later. I tried to get some rest and help my body heal, but the pain kept getting worse as time progressed.

About a month later, I was in agony. Constant pain was shooting throughout my back, hips, neck, legs and arms. I was nauseous and having problems with bladder incontinence.

There were times when the pain was so bad that I couldn't take care of myself properly. I couldn't wash dishes, fold laundry, do up buttons, or even put my own pants on, because every time I moved the agony would come shooting up through my limbs.

As the months wore on, the pain became all-consuming. It could push me out of my mind, making it impossible to focus on anything else. I lost my job in HR soon after the incident because I couldn't concentrate on anything, and it hurt so much just to move. It was completely unlike me to be helpless and dependant. Being incapable of even carrying out life's basic actions really took a toll on my self-esteem.

Pain is a very difficult thing to measure. You go to doctors and they ask you to rate your pain on a scale of 1 to 10, but what does that mean? It's so subjective. I knew of someone who committed suicide to get relief from her own chronic pain, and yet she had never qualified for a disability. I admit there were days when I thought that the only way I could ever be rid of my pain was through death, but I was lucky because I didn't want to die. I had Al and many other loving friends and family who made life worth living – sources of joy that the pain couldn't take away from me.

After many consultations with doctors and specialists, I finally got into the hospital to have a spinal surgery on May 30, 2004, a whole four months after the collision. The doctors still didn't know exactly what was wrong with me at that point, which only served to increase my stress levels prior to the procedure and make the pain worse than ever.

I was hospitalized about a week prior to the operation so that I could be stabilized before the surgery. Once I was ready, the surgeons performed what is called a "laminectomy" on my spine, which in simplified terms means they removed two vertebrae and took out a calcified cyst that had been pinching and rubbing against my spinal cord, and then replaced the two bones in my back. The procedure effectively fixed my thoracic spine, but the vertebral column in my neck was still almost a half inch out of alignment from when it had broken while absorbing the shock of the initial impact.

I spent another week in the hospital recovering after the surgery, then proceeded to work through six months of one-to-one therapy at the Eastern Ontario Trauma Rehabilitation Centre, followed by 12 months of water therapy exercises done on my own in a pool according to a plan the therapists gave me. Thanks to this treatment and the surgery, I was able to regain control of my bladder and the pain in my legs was greatly reduced.

I'd been on all kinds of medication before the operation, but it wasn't until 18 months after that they found the right kind of meds to suit my needs. Those months were a hard time in my life, and I have to give Al credit for helping me through them while I slept a lot and didn't emerge much from my depressed state.

Toward the end of this difficult time I decided that I couldn't just cater to my pain all day. I had to stop letting it get to me. It might hurt physically to go out and live my life like before, but if I didn't get out of the house, then what did it matter if I was in pain or not? My life was still passing me by.

I think finding the right meds and a positive outlook are what allowed me to keep on pushing forward. Today, taking my medication in a perfect world, the pain should be under control. Sadly, we don't live in a perfect world. Any time I get sick, stressed, overtired, or upset my body in any other way, there comes the pain again, coursing back through my limbs and torso.

Prior to the surgery, the doctors told me that I would most likely never be able to work again, and recommended that we downsize the house to make it more accessible; they feared my condition would worsen with age.

We had a fair bit of land in Verona, so we decided to parcel off a piece of our property and build a new, smaller, more accessible house on it, and fund the new house's construction by selling off the rest of our property and my old dreamhouse.

This meant that after coming out of my operation, I didn't even have a house to come home to – I had to stay in a hotel for a few months while the contractors finished building our new little home.

Moving to a new house wasn't the only plate to shift under my feet after my accident. I had to go to a psychologist to learn to grieve the athletic life I was now being forced to leave behind. It was so hard to let go of such an important part of who I was. Where once I had been proud of my physical and mental strength as an athlete, now

I could hardly move my body and my once clear mind was fogged up with medication.

I could no longer kayak or swim after the incident, because the strong arm and core movements would only have provoked waves of agony at each stroke. I couldn't run or bike because the jostling on the run would have sent knives up my back and my neck wasn't strong enough to hold my head up over the handlebars of my tri bike. I couldn't bring myself to stand in our laneway when the new owners came to pick up my beloved kayak, and I wasn't able to go through the process of selling my tri bike myself – I had to get my niece Terri to handle the operation on my behalf.

This situation probably came to a peak a few weeks after getting out of the hospital, when my girlfriend Jenine Davy took me to see the movie *Million Dollar Baby*, directed by Clint Eastwood, about a female boxer who becomes paralyzed and loses the will to live. After the show I sat in the car and sobbed because, like Hilary Swank in the movie, I broke down and truly grieved the life I was walking away from.

Poor Jenine was so good to me – being a nurse, she asked if my pain had escalated. I realized that my physical suffering was under control, but I was still experiencing heartbreak from having to say goodbye to my life as an athlete.

It seems that the only form of physical activity I had left was walking. The doctors recommended that I keep walking as often as I could, and suggested that I might get a dog to accompany me and make sure I walked every day. This led to the acquisition of my dog

Brandy, who was not only a great walking buddy, but also a sort of solace and joy for me whenever I had a bad day:

The doctors actually gave me a special note so that I could bring Brandy into hotels, restaurants, wherever I went. In a way, Brandy was like a therapy dog for me, even in an era when therapy dogs were not as common as they are today. She was an important part of my rehabilitation – a simple comfort in my new, less colourful life.

I admit that I found it deeply ironic that someone as passionate about safety and hockey as I was could end up suffering life-altering injuries from an unfortunate collision while playing the game that I love. But it was even more ironic to discover that the insurance money I had provided for girls in hockey (by getting our tournament sanctioned by the CAHA [Hockey Canada's precursor] in 1982) was now being withheld from me in my time of need.

Indeed, Hockey Canada's insurance policy was such that I didn't qualify for anything more than $5,000 in damages because I wasn't paraplegic or quadriplegic. I could still technically move my limbs, and the association didn't take into consideration the fact that I had lost my job, had to sell my house, had to pay for expensive therapy, or most importantly, that I was still suffering from spinal trauma and severely debilitating pain.

When I learned this news, I was mad. It felt like almost everything I cared about in life had been taken away from me, and I wasn't getting compensation to pay for the proper support and care I needed to make the best of an already deplorable situation.

175

I talked to representatives from Hockey Canada and asked if there was any way I could receive more coverage for my injury. They told me that, legally, the only way I could hope to get the money I needed was to sue the player who had hit me, and trigger *her* Hockey Canada insurance coverage since she would be protected from being sued by the association. So that was what I did.

I deeply regret all the emotional trauma and judicial hassle that I had to put this poor lady through just to get money for treatment and to replace my lost income. I'm sure she felt very victimized throughout the whole ordeal, and rightfully so. But I was left with very few other options to choose from, and in the end, I am only human.

This woman was a necessary gateway to get to the real culprit, Hockey Canada, who had refused to give money for players suffering "immeasurable" injuries like debilitating pain and concussions. Nowadays, thankfully, doctors have come up with better systems to diagnose and monitor concussions, such as baseline cognitive testing, which can be used to measure brain damage by comparing test scores before and after a hit.

Without these technologies however, Hockey Canada was able to argue that rewarding claims such as mine would only serve to make their hockey programs financially "prohibitive" for less wealthy families. While this is perhaps a good point, they didn't take into consideration the negative impact that *not* rewarding claims like this could have on future families down the line.[62]

Although I was never able to go back to hockey, triathlon, kayaking or any other sports, I made progress in my recovery throughout the years that even my doctors hadn't thought possible. Recently, I have been able to go for a few short skates around local rinks, although certainly not as lithely as before, and I really pay for it the day after! But most importantly, I was able to return to work about 8 years after that ill-fated collision.

Most people don't realize how much of a privilege it is to be able to work and earn your own living. It provides you with distraction and fulfillment that everyone should get to have in their life.

By 2012, I had become accustomed to living with my pain, and I thought that I would like to try working a little bit again if I could. My niece Debbie owned the successful business *HR.com* that I had been working for before my injury, and she was kind enough to let me take my time and start back as slowly as I needed to. I started off working just 12 to 15 hours a week as a facilitator for the Quality of Hire Community in her business.

Six years after that, things were going well, and I decided to change jobs to work at *advos*, another company in the HR sector. It was then that I started working again full time, now as Vice President

---

[62] Nonetheless, this is all the more reason to take this opportunity to donate to your local sports programs like the Grindstone Award Foundation, which helps give girls in poorer families the chance to play such a wonderful sport.

of advos. I made it very clear to my new boss Mark that I didn't know how well it would go working full time because of the difficulty I had moving and concentrating, but he said that he was willing to take a chance on me. Since then, Mark has told me that I have even exceeded the expectations he set out for me, a fact which makes me extremely proud.

This is where I am today. My dog Brandy has since passed on and been replaced by another wonderful therapy puppy, Abby. I have a great job with caring people supporting me who know my limits, and I'm at peace knowing I'm giving back to society. I have a bright future full of dog walks and other joys ahead of me. And most importantly, I have an incredible husband whom I love deeply and who has been unconditionally by my side through all the trauma and hardship. Despite the pain, I am making the best of my current situation.

Reflections on the Past
& Thoughts for the Future

One of the best parts of sifting through old memories to find nuggets of stories from the past is that the practice allows us to better reflect on the future. In women's hockey, our trials have been long and laborious, and I'm sure the future holds many further challenges before we reach true equality with the men, not only in sport but also in the world at large. And so to you, future generations of strong young women and their supporters, I pass the torch.

It is my most sincere wish that this story will help you to understand what you're up against, what we've been facing since the start. This wish what gave me the courage to write a memoir. I hope my memoir will give you the courage to continue our battle.

A lot of thought has gone into the creation of this book. I won't lie to you; I was worried that it might be seen as a vanity project, or that old-fashioned individuals might dismiss it as no more than "ill-founded, typical feminist man-hating." But I felt that I had to share my story for the sake of young women today, whether you're battling discrimination in the sports world or elsewhere.

I share my story to give voice to all those who have been thrown unexpected obstacles in life, but who found it within themselves to keep on pushing, and to document the details and struggles of women's hockey in Canada in a forgotten but important period of our past.

The challenge with writing a memoir is that everyone remembers things differently – everyone's memories are coloured through their own biases and past experiences. When things aren't officially recorded or documented, it can be difficult to find the "truth" of a story, if there even is such a thing. To mitigate the biases in this memoir, I have done my best to call around and ask my friends from the era about their experiences in the beginning days of women's hockey, to try and corroborate my story and sort out any blurry details if I could.

Sometimes, however, this method is impractical since I have lost contact with many of my companions, and many have since passed. Thus, there are places in the book where I had to rely on my memories alone. Please forgive me, then, if I have committed any errors unknowingly, and write me a note so that I may correct them.[63]

There are a few people, such as my old friend John Munro, who have apologized recently for not giving women in hockey the assistance we needed at the time. This small act of recognition really

[63] Please write to rhondaal@rogers.com.

meant a lot to me. There are many people who have made mistakes in the past due to uncritically following the customs of the post-war era, but now know that it is never too late to make a change.

It is also important to recognize that concessions are difficult for those in the wrong, especially when someone had no idea that they were committing an error in the first place. We need to be patient with people who still adhere to old-fashioned doctrines and calmly explain to them exactly why something is wrong instead of bursting out in anger and accusations. This is the best way to achieve the cultural shift needed to see the eradication of sexism in future generations.

In the wake of the folding of the CWHL (Canadian Women's Hockey League) in May 2019, it can be difficult to keep a positive outlook when the future of women in sports seems to be sliding downhill.[64] Here is hoping that the NWHL (the National [American] Women's Hockey League) will expand to include all the lost players of the CWHL and create an effective counterpart to the NHL for women across the world, similar to the WNBA or the NWSL but with equal pay. Experts like Dr. Julie Stevens believe this may in fact represent a better opportunity for professional female hockey players in the future.[65]

[64] Stelter, Brian. "US viewers tuned into women's World Cup final in record numbers." *CNN Business*, 8 July 2019, www.cnn.com/2019/07/08/media/womens-world-cup-tv-ratings/index.html. Accessed 16 July 2019.

[65] Stevens, Julie. "The death of the CWHL presents a new opportunity for women's professional hockey," *National Post*, 4 Apr. 2019, https://nationalpost.com/pmn/news-pmn/the-death-of-the-cwhl-presents-a-new-opportunity-for-womens-professional-hockey. Accessed 15 Sept. 2019.

Unlike the CWHL, the NWHL pays their players a minimum salary of $5,000 per player, which is a laughable sum next to the millions and millions of dollars allocated to NHL players each season, but we must remember that it is progress nonetheless.

If we want to truly see equality in professional hockey, we need to have two parallel mirrored programs where both men and women receive equal funding, equal playing opportunities, and equal media coverage and hype.[66] Many argue that women, being in general less physically "fast and strong" than men, don't deserve the same kinds of programs as their male counterparts, who are seen as more impressive and thus "TV-worthy."

To this, I answer that these critics would be surprised at what physical feats a woman can accomplish if she is given the same amount of training time and resources as the men currently enjoy, and how well-received by the public her game would be if she was given the same crowd-exciting media promotion as her brothers. We're already beginning to challenge this reputation, with recent advances such as in the Women's FIFA World Cup, where the American women enjoyed a greater television audience in the USA than their male counterparts, despite still being paid less than the men.[67]

---

[66] I chose to address only the condition of women in this memoir for the sake of maintaining a focused scope, and because I don't pretend to have the expertise or knowledge required to provide appropriate insight into the even greater difficulties faced by transgender individuals and all other non-binary femmes. These domains are worthy of in-depth studies all their own.
[67] "Women's World Cup: Record-breaking numbers," *BBC News,* 8 July 2019, https://www.bbc.com/news/world-48882465. Accessed 18 Sept. 2019.

I believe that by focusing on the growth of minor girls' hockey leagues and developing a positive image of women athletes, we can foster the next generation of strong, empowered NWHL players who will put women's hockey on the prime spot every second Saturday night.

In terms of economics, it is the women who make 80% of all consumer decisions on goods and services available in North America.[68] This means that we already have the power to influence the sport market to our advantage and put incredible female athletes on our screens. These healthy role models will, in turn, inspire even more young women in the next generation to become better athletes and better citizens.

Moreover, I think many would be surprised at what changes we could accomplish if we were to take legal body contact completely out of both the men and women's programs. This would take the focus of hockey away from the goonish violence and back to the impressive mental and physical skill that make it such an amazing game. Remember that the original six NHL teams deployed no gladiator-esque checking like today since the old-style equipment didn't allow for that kind of barbarism, and instead forced players to focus more on the finesse of the sport.

Not only would removing body contact serve to make a safer and healthier game for all involved (as the McMurtry Report proved

---

[68] "FEMALE CONSUMERISM: What Women Want." *Brand Strategy*, 2006, p. 40. *ProQuest*,
https://proxy.library.mcgill.ca/login?url=https://search.proquest.com/docview/224186372?accountid=12339.

as early as 1974), but it would also help to drastically close the gap between the levels of competition in male and female play, making the female sport more marketable and profitable for its female athletes. This would create a positive feedback cycle that would again enable women hockey players to devote their efforts to their training, and produce even greater advances in the quality of their play.

Let it also be noted that we women are an incredible sex in our own right – although many denounce us as being "weaker" than men, women actually hold most of the overall records in ultramarathon running and marathon swimming, because of our superior ability to use fat as an energy source compared to men. It is a shame that most of today's more popular team sports don't cater to the strength sets of women, although perhaps this too will change in the future.

Team sports for girls are vitally important in today's society, because they teach the exact character and skill sets that young women need to be empowered later on in life when they enter the workforce. Traits such as collaboration, communication, risk analysis, work ethic, and courage are all taught on the field or the rink, and are exactly what young women today need to be able to push for and achieve pay equity.

Hardly surprising, then, that a recent study found 90% of high-level female executives were involved in sports in their youth.[69]

[69] "Women Athletes Business Network – Perspectives on sport and teams," *Ernst & Young*, May 2013, https://www.ey.com/br/pt/about-us/our-sponsorships-and-programs/women-athletes-global-leadership-network---perspectives-on-sport-and-teams. Accessed 14 Aug. 2019.

This is why I believe sport is so important. We need to inspire, equip, and prepare the women of our future.

Another study examined the demographics of the CEOs of 1500 of the top companies across North America, and found that there are more men named John than the total number of women in these positions. [70] That fact is unacceptable, and proves exactly why it is so essential that we empower ourselves and the next generation of capable women to finally break through the glass ceilings that have been holding us back for far too long.

As women, we need to be the leaders in the battle against gender inequality, whether it is in sport or elsewhere. But we also need to demand that men take action alongside us, because we cannot win the game if only half the team is playing.

Words are the strongest weapon I know. I have shared with you my story. Now I ask you in return to go out and use your power, your discourse, your competence, to enact real change for the next generation.

Let's level the playing field.

[70] Wolfers, Justin. "Fewer Women Run Big Companies Than Men Named John," *The New York Times,* 2 Mar 2015, https://www.nytimes.com/2015/03/03/upshot/fewer-women-run-big-companies-than-men-named-john.html?mcubz=0. Accessed 13 Aug. 2019.

Acknowledgements

I would personally like to thank all the people who have helped to make this passion book into a reality. First of all, I would like to thank John Hollon and Laurie Milner for advising us through the publishing process and using up their free time to edit our manuscript. I would also like to thank Jeff Greco for creating our beautiful website (check it out: www.rhondaleemantaylor.com), and Marlon Lahens for the incredible art work on our cover, promotional posters, and at chapter heads throughout the book. Finally, I would like to thank Peter Singh-Vigilante for putting all the pieces together and finalizing the layout of the book.

Eric Anderson, Keith Thompson, Clive Powell, John Munro, Jill Breugem, and Hugo Schutzberg also deserve recognition for their invaluable support and their help in guiding us through the publishing process. Many thanks to Paul Patskouin and David McCallum for donating their valuable time and video skills. I also appreciate the input from Carl Noble, Joey Bush, Michel Vigneault, Cookie Cartwright, and my brothers Ed and Glenn Leeman, who helped to clarify blurry details from the past and offer their own perspectives on the history of women's hockey in Canada. Thank you also to Mark Willaman from *advos* for saving us thousands of dollars by giving us free use of his amazing marketing platform, and to Tatjana "Tiki" Tikhonov, Denyse Lafrance Horning, Julie Stevens, and Jane Lagacé for taking the time to review and excerpts for our manuscript, and support our cause in many other ways.

Finally, I would like to thank my husband Al Taylor for his continued love and support throughout the ups and downs of the writing and publishing process. He has been my guiding light, and believed in me every step of the way.

Thank you all. This book would not have been possible without all these wonderful people!

Appendix A

[Transcript: *I don't think you're a real hockey player at all. / Prove to me that you're a real hockey player. / You're a real hockey player!*]

A drawing by Cookie, with us as hockey-playing Peanuts' characters sporting gaping grins. To add to the list of her many talents, Cookie is now an amateur artist.

Appendix B

A poster sold at the first Women's Nationals, 1982. The same image was used as the cover page for the programs and flyers distributed for the tournament.

Appendix C

The Shoppers Tournament logo featured at centre ice as well as on
pamphlets, banners, posters, and the plaque attached to trophy.

Appendix D

Government of Canada
Fitness and Amateur Sport

Gouvernement du Canada
Condition physique et Sport amateur

365 Laurier Ave. West
Ottawa, Ontario
KIA OX6

March 16, 1982

Rhonda Leeman
Tournament Chairperson
OWHA
160 Vanderhoof
Toronto, Ontario

The First National Women's Ice Hockey Championship Tournament represents a milestone for sport in Canada. However unofficial the title may be, there is no doubt that Canadians have long recognized ice hockey as "the national game".

It is equally true that "the national game" has afforded relatively few opportunities for participation by girls and women. There have been occasional bursts of activity as long ago as the early years of this century and there were major tournaments over forty years ago at which a Dominion Ladies Championship team was declared.

But the 1982 Tournament represents the first genuinely national event for female hockey players, and the Tournament symbolizes as well the fact that women's hockey has come of age.

We will, no doubt, hear about a great many more Gail Cummings', but even as we do, we can remain confident that issue for women's hockey is not whether it will grow and develop but how it will grow.

To the tournament organizers who had foresight to persevere under difficult circumstances, and to the players and coaches who will make this Tournament and important athletic event, Sport Canada extends best wishes for a successful weekend and a bright future for women's hockey in Canada.

Abby Hoffman

Canadä

A letter I received from Abby Hoffman at Sport Canada during the first Women's Nationals in 1982.

Appendix E

The Huntsville Honey Pin given out to the RIK Danish exchange

team, 1983.[71]

Appendix F

I'M A HOCKEY PLAYER

St. Peter stood at the Pearly Gates,
As three female athletes their turn did wait.
"What did you do?" asked St. Peter to the first in line.

"I was a swimmer with the best of time.
I swam for Canada, I swam my best;
I gained recognition from east to west."

"Oh, what a life you must have had,
The glory, the countries, the people you've met.
Step aside and let me see,
Who you have in your company."

The next in line was dressed so nice.
St. Peter claimed, "Your duds are of high price."

"Don't worry," she claimed,
"Tennis was my game.
A hundred here a thousand there,
Given to me just for being there."

"Oh, I am terribly impressed.
However, let's see who is next."

"I played hockey," piped up the third.
"Even though my parents thought it quite absurd.
Getting up at 5:00 a.m., borrowing equipment from my brother,
Was the ritual to get out on the ice along with the others.
No money I gained, I am not known.
Believe me, St. Peter, the happiness brought cannot be shown."

"The frustrations endured you've handled them well,
Being involved in female hockey has been your stint in hell."

Transcript of a poignant poem on women's hockey published in a 1980 OWHA Newsletter. Author unknown.

Bibliography

Adams, Carly, and Julie Stevens. "Change and grassroots movement: re-conceptiualizing women's hockey governance in Canada," *Int. J. Sport Management and Merketing,* vol. 2, no. 4, 2007, pp. 344-361.

Almeida SA, et al. "Gender Differences in Musculoskeletal Injury Rates: A Function of Symptom Reporting?" *Medicine and Science in Sports and Exercise,* vol. 31, no. 12, 1999, pp. 1807–1812.

The Associated Press. "Viktor Tikhonov, legendary Soviet Union hockey coach, dead at 84." *CBC Sports,* 24 Nov. 2014, www.cbc.ca/sports/hockey/nhl/viktor-tikhonov-legendary-soviet-union-hockey-coach-dead-at-84-1.2846640. Accessed 16 July 2019.

Avery, Joanna, and Julie Anne Stevens. *Too Many Men on the Ice: Women's Hockey in North America.* Polestar Book, 1997. Print.

Bolender, Keith. "Girls' hockey? They're proving the game can be played just for fun," *The Toronto Star* [Toronto], Oct. 7 1980.

Brown, Susan. "Slapshot! It's their turn on the ice," *Detroit Free Press* [Detroit], 1 Feb. 1982.

Etue, Elizabeth, and Megan K. Williams. *On the Edge: Women Making Hockey History.* EPUB ed., Toronto, Second Story Press, 1999. Print.

"FEMALE CONSUMERISM: What Women Want." *Brand Strategy,* 2006, pp. 40. *ProQuest,* https://proxy.library.mcgill.ca/login?url=https://search.proquest.com/docview/224186372?accountid=12339.

Flegg, Erin. "Final days of a hockey legacy," *The Queen's Journalit should,* 5 Apr. 2007, https://www.queensjournal.ca/story/2007-04-05/news/final-days-hockey-legacy/. Accessed 16 Sept. 2019.

"Girls on Ice – Finally," in *Take Thirty, CBC,* 17 Feb. 1983, https://www.cbc.ca/player/play/1586099799. Video. Accessed 7 Sept. 2019.

Hall, M. Ann. *The Girl and the Game,* University of Toronto Press, 2017.

Hall, M. Ann, and Dorothy A. Richardson. *Fair Ball: Towards Sex Equality in Canadian Sport.* Ottawa, Canadian Advisory Council on the Status of Women, 1982. Print.

"History," *Rivulettes Junior Hockey Club,* Cambridge City Archives, http://rivuletteshockey.pointstreaksites.com/view/rivuletteshockey/history. Accessed 1 Sept. 2019.

"History of Ringette." *Ringette Canada,* www.ringette.ca/our-sport/history-of-ringette/. Accessed 28 May 2019.

"Hockey Canada Annual Report." *Hockey Canada*, June 2017, cdn.hockeycanada.ca/hockeycanada/Corporate/About/Downloads/2016-17-annual-report-e.pdf. Accessed 29 June 2019.

Horner, Matina. *Sex Differences in Achievement Motivation and Performance in Competitive and Non-Competitive Situations.* Ph.D. Dissertation, University of Michigan, 1968.

Hunter, Andria. "Hockey Registration in Canada." *The Women's Hockey Web*, www.whockey.com/country/canada/registration.html. Accessed 29 June 2019.

Lafrance Horning, Denyse. "Women's Recreational Hockey: A New Player Profile," in Ellison, Jenny, and Jennifer Anderson, editors. *Hockey : Challenging Canada's Game, Au-Delà Du Sport National.* Canadian Museum of History, 2018. *Project Muse*, https://muse-jhu-edu.proxy3.library.mcgill.ca/chapter/2109396. Accessed 13 Sept. 2019.

Manning, Sally. *A Golden Tear: Danièle Sauvageau's Journey to Olympic Gold.* Toronto, CNIB, 2004.

Massport Jets Records. Schlesinger Library, Radcliffe Institute. Harvard Library, https://hollis.harvard.edu/primo-explore/fulldisplay?docid=01HVD_ALMA212032117760003941&context=L&vid=HVH2&lang=en_US&search_scope=everything&adaptor=Local%20Search%20Engine&tab=everything&query=any,contains,massport%20jets&offset=0. Accessed 15 Oct. 2019.

McConnell, Wendy. "Honeys work and effort pay off in Denmark." *The Forester* [Huntsville], 9 Mar. 1983.

McFarlane, Brian. *Proud Past, Bright Future: One Hundred Years of Canadian Women's Hockey.* Toronto, Stoddart, 1994. Print.

McKenzie, Robert. "Hockey for Girls Gains Momentum." *The Globe and Mail* [Toronto], 22 Sept. 1981.

McMurtry, William R. "Investigation and Inquiry into Violence in Amateur Hockey," 4 Oct. 1974. Report. http://www.ontla.on.ca/library/repository/mon/25005/32920.pdf. Accessed 7 Sept. 2019.

Norris, Mike. "Queen's goalie made history by donning mask," *The Kingston Whig Standard* [Kingston], 19 Feb. 2016, https://www.thewhig.com/2016/02/19/queens-goalie-made-history-by-donning-mask/wcm/9f40a766-8200-3fd4-8faa-fd207c51974d. Accessed 3 Sept. 2019.

Power, Tracey. *Glory.* 26 July 2019, Thousand Islands Playhouse. Theatrical Performance.

Rhonie Horne, quoted in Scanlon, Kevin. "Sibling Rivalry Can Inspire Girls on Ice," *The Toronto Star* [Toronto], 20 Dec. 1981.

Riseboro, Caroline. "Why we're Losing Ground in the Fight for Gender Equality," *YouTube,* Ted Talk, https://www.youtube.com/watch?v=lRCioDtwpRc. Accessed 13 Sept. 2019.

Rivers, Caryl. "The Girls of Summer: All the Dirt on the American Tomboy or Why Girls Say To Heck with the Prince- I'll Keep the Frog," *womenSports,* 1977.

Stelter, Brian. "US viewers tuned into women's World Cup final in record numbers." *CNN Business*, 8 July 2019, www.cnn.com/2019/07/08/media/womens-world-cup-tv-ratings/index.html. Accessed 16 July 2019.

Stevens, Julie. "The death of the CWHL presents a new opportunity for women's professional hockey," *National Post*, 4 Apr. 2019, https://nationalpost.com/pmn/news-pmn/the-death-of-the-cwhl-presents-a-new-opportunity-for-womens-professional-hockey. Accessed 15 Sept. 2019.

Vigneault, Michel. *La Naissance d'un sport organisé au Canada: le hockey à Montéal, 1875-1917.* Ph.D. Dissertation, Université Laval, Quebec, July 2001.

Wolfers, Justin. "Fewer Women Run Big Companies Than Men Named John," *The New York Times* [New York], 2 March 2015, https://www.nytimes.com/2015/03/03/upshot/fewer-women-run-big-companies-than-men-named-john.html?mcubz=0. Accessed 13 Aug. 2019.

"Women Athletes Business Network – Perspectives on sport and teams," *Ernst & Young*, May 2013, https://www.ey.com/br/pt/about-us/our-sponsorships-and-programs/women-athletes-global-leadership-network---perspectives-on-sport-and-teams. Accessed 14 Aug. 2019.

"Women's World Cup: Record-breaking numbers," *BBC News,* 8 July 2019, https://www.bbc.com/news/world-48882465. Accessed 18 Sept. 2019.

CPSIA information can be obtained
at www.ICGtesting.com
Printed in the USA
LVHW012117210721
693314LV00016B/1750